Library

Small Livestock Housing

A Construction Guide

Small Livestock Housing

A Construction Guide

Joe Jacobs

THE CROWOOD PRESS

First published in 2010 by
The Crowood Press Ltd
Ramsbury, Marlborough
Wiltshire SN8 2HR

www.crowood.com

British Library Cataloguing-in-Publication Data
A catalogue record for this book is available from the British Library.

ISBN 978 1 84797 188 3

Disclaimer
Power tools and other tools and equipment used to produce small
livestock housing are potentially dangerous and it is vitally important
that they are used in strict accordance with both the current health
and safety regulations and the manufacturer's instructions. The
author and the publisher do not accept any responsibility in any
manner whatsoever for any error or omission, or any loss, damage,
injury, adverse outcome, or liability of any kind incurred as a result of
the use of any of the information contained in this book, or reliance
upon it. If in doubt about any aspect of constructing small livestock
housing readers are advised to seek professional advice.

Acknowledgements
Thanks to all those who did my farm work whilst I sat on my PC
fussing about what to write.

All photographs and line-drawings by the author.

Typeset by D & N Publishing, Baydon, Wiltshire.
Printed and bound in Malaysia by Times Offset (M) Sdn Bhd.

Contents

Introduction

I vividly remember the first time I saw an advert in a newspaper offering battery hens for retirement at the grand sum of fifty pence each. The trouble was, where to put them? After collecting those first birds, very little time passed before our flock started to expand. Within months we had decided to try our hand at breeding poultry. Along with our growing collection of birds, came a growing need for bird housing. Whilst we do not berate the manufacturers of very nice-looking poultry housing, the cost of some commercially made poultry and small-animal housing is plainly excessive. With an ambitious breeding programme in mind, it took little time at all for me to realize that I would have to design and build my own. In the ensuing years, vast quantities of home-made poultry and animal houses have been made and destroyed, and have graced the pages of books and magazines. Many of the constructions still exist in one guise or another, others have returned to carbon, some deservedly so. I never set out in life to be a DIY writer; come to think of it, I didn't set out to be a pig farmer either but through my inadvertent enthusiasm for making, breaking and modifying things, I hope that a little of what I have done might inspire you to try some projects of your own. Hopefully you will find out that DIY can be fun.

THE RIGHT TOOLS FOR THE JOB

Many of the projects in this book can be built with a very basic set of tools. The major headache for the DIY-oriented author is that if I made one of everything using nothing but simple hand tools, it would barely be possible to get around to actually writing a book. In recent years, the cost of reasonable quality power tools has dropped so low that for such project work as this, it is impractical not to own them. I will endeavour to stress that the projects can be made without power tools but it takes a lot longer. I'd certainly suggest, as a minimum, that an electric drill, a sander and a jigsaw should be obtained prior to starting work.

The following additional hand tools will be needed to complete the projects:

- A hammer – I prefer a medium-weight claw hammer.
- Screwdrivers – a selection of cross and flat heads with decent quality tips.
- Saws – a basic 51cm (20in) panel saw. If you haven't got an electric jigsaw, you'll need a coping or key-hole saw for cutting curves.
- Drill – as cited, an electric drill and a selection of drill bits between 2 and 10mm (0.08–0.39in).
- Pencil – for marking out your project work.

- Tape – a 5m (16.4ft) retractable tape is a must for quickly marking out large sheets of wood.
- Straight edge – this does not have to be a graduated ruler, as long as it is straight.
- Sandpaper and a sanding block – buy a pack of sandpaper with a selection of grades.
- Surform or plane – can be used to smooth rough edges and remove excess timber.

Other Useful Power Tools

Without getting into the realms of bench-mounted and fixed woodworking tools, there are a few other powered devices that can be used to expedite the construction process. A circular saw is very useful for cutting up large sheets of plywood. As many of the projects in this book stem from large sheets of ply, a circular saw is desirable but by no means necessary; you can do the job with a jigsaw. There are two or three types of electric sander available. A sheet sander is handy for finishing rough edges and small areas. If you have a lot of surplus material that needs removing, then you really need a belt sander. The problem with a belt sander is that if you are not zealous enough, you may find that your machine has eaten away a fair bit more than you desired.

Working Safely

It is worth mentioning that having the right tools for the job also means ones that are well-lubricated, sharp and in good working condition. Anything less will only fuel the chain of events that ends with an accident. When working with power tools of any sort, you need to be aware of their limitations and wear appropriate safety equipment. As there are often accidents where hapless power-tool wielders have cut through their own cable, make sure your electrical system is fitted with an RCD (Residual Current Device) that will (hopefully) cut the power in the event of a mishap. If you don't have an RCD, you can get an in-line one or an extension reel with one already fitted.

Goggles, ear-defenders, a dust mask and gloves are all to be found ready to hand in my workshop. As a farmer, I wear steel toe-cap rigger boots and overalls, which offer some protection against DIY pitfalls. Even with basic projects, you need to take steps to ensure your personal health and safety.

SUITABLE MATERIALS AND WHERE TO FIND THEM

Most of the projects in the book use relatively simple construction techniques with a limited choice of materials. For most of the projects we are going to use a combination of plywood and 50 × 25mm (2 × 1in) treated roofing battens. The main reason for doing this is that they are both readily available from any timber or builder's merchant or any large DIY emporium. The secondary motive is that both of these materials are inexpensive, so it doesn't matter if you

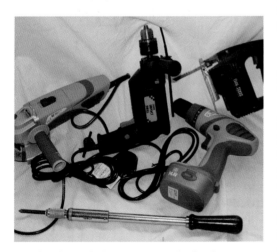

A selection of cheap power tools that get the job done a lot quicker. Note the very useful Yankee Screwdriver.

make a mistake. If you feel that you would like to substitute a better quality timber into your projects, go right ahead.

Plywood is available in many grades and thicknesses. I'd suggest using 9mm ³⁄₈in thick plywood for most of these projects. The next grade up is 12mm ½in, which does come in handy for larger, heavier projects. When it comes to the quality of the timber available, there are generally three grades of outdoor plywood that are applicable to us:

- At the top end of the spectrum is marine ply: quality glue and quality laminations make up an engineered timber that is resilient to water and looks good.
- The middle grade of ply will have at least one good hardwood face and reasonable quality laminations.
- Shuttering ply is the very yellow, knotty looking plywood with only one half-decent face. Shuttering ply is the least pricey of the grades; that said, if it's treated well and the treatment is worked into the edges, it will still last an ample length of time.

Plywood is still manufactured to imperial sizes and is best purchased in large 2.5 × 1.22m (8 × 4ft) sheets. Many timber yards and DIY stores have a large cutter and can chop up a sheet for you for a pound or two extra, so that it will fit in your auto. Go to the shops prepared with your plans, so that you don't get home with nicely chopped-up pieces that are too small.

WOODWORKING TECHNIQUES

Anyone who did woodwork or metalwork at school, before the powers that be deemed it overly dangerous, might have learnt the difference between a dovetail and a mitre. If you study modern construction techniques, especially of furniture, it does not take long to spot that many of the traditional methods have gone in the bin in favour of metal and plastic fixings. The simplest form of joint is where one piece of timber rests (or is butted up) against another. Sorry to disappoint anyone who had visions of complex woodwork but the majority of readers will not have the equipment for overly complex projects. We'll be sticking with the humble butt joint and a minimum level of difficulty.

Usage of Measurements

Throughout the book we'll be giving measurements in both metric and imperial forms. As the projects were by and large designed in metric, imperial figures listed may end up seeming a bit random. The pedants amongst us may even note that some imperial measurements are up to an eighth of an inch away from their metric counterparts. In instances of such variation as described, I've only rounded the imperial measurement either way if I thought that the project could stand it without significant visual or material defect. If you are building a project in metric, stay in metric; if you are working in imperial, stay in imperial.

Sanding and Finishing

Throughout the book you will find that scant regard is given to the preparation of components other than cutting them to size. Obviously, if you have just cut a component and it has a particularly rough edge, it will want a little sanding to improve the quality of the finish. As you work through any particular project, try and finish each component to a reasonable standard and you will vastly improve the overall quality of the project.

Chapter 1

Basic Chicken House

GETTING STARTED WITH POULTRY

In recent times there has been something of a renaissance in backyard poultry keeping, and rightly so. When much of our food is shipped for daft distances, we have barely a clue where it comes from. There has never been a better time to have home-laid eggs, right on your doorstep. Chickens are addictive. Not only are they available in a huge variety of colours, shapes and sizes, but they have entertaining personalities to match; get two and you'll soon want twenty. A gift of a few fresh eggs can quickly win over friends and enemies alike; on occasions, eggs are even a useful bartering tool. The argument

You can keep poultry for pleasure, profit or even competition.

'What will we do when we go away on holiday?' doesn't wash. You'll soon have a queue of would-be chicken-minders who'll look after the flock in exchange for the eggs. Of course chickens can also be kept for meat, showing, breeding or even ornamental purposes. Hopefully some readers might graduate to life beyond eggs, after they've picked up their tools and built their first chicken house.

Build Your Own House

You may have elected to pick up this book because you already have chickens; you may have opened the book because you want to keep poultry but need to make somewhere suitable for them to live. What comes first? The chicken or the shed? Arguably, it's the shed. In order to keep chickens you need a secure house that is resilient to the weather, offers protection from foxes and other vermin, and offers the birds a clean environment in which they can sleep, nest and lay their eggs.

If in your quest to house poultry, you've gone as far as looking at commercially available housing, it will already have hit you that it is not cheap; in fact, much of it is downright expensive. The answer inevitably is to manufacture your own. Hopefully this chapter will aid you, the tool holder, to craft a chicken house at a modest price that will keep your birds warm, dry and happy for many years to come.

The Chicken House Design

Further on in your investigations you may have noted that chicken house architecture varies from the understated to the ridiculous. Whilst ornate designs are very nice, our order of the day is to create a house that is both functional and relatively easy to manufacture. The two basic designs of chicken house are the triangular shape, known as an ark, or the familiar 'lean-to' sloping roof shape. In this instance we are going to take the basic, easy-to-manufacture chicken ark and modify it with the addition of nesting compartments and perches for the birds. What we will end up with, hopefully, is a house that will accommodate six birds.

For those that have never kept poultry, it may upset you to know that they can be extremely destructive if left to their own devices in a nice garden. I tend to keep birds incarcerated during the growing months and let them free-range in the colder weather. This way, we do at least get a decent crop of vegetables and flowers. With this is mind, during the process of working out a fresh design for this project, I decided to make the system modular. The initial project has a small run attached that can be used as a temporary (short-term) pen; it would suffice if you were going to get back home after dark and there was no-one around to shut the birds up. If you require a larger run, you will be able to move on to the next project in the following chapter. Combining the first two projects in the book will provide you with a chicken house that has an enclosure that could be used on a permanent basis.

With poultry houses, cleanliness is a major issue and so the house needs to be as easy to muck out as possible. With this in mind, we have opted to design a house that has a side that can be completely opened up. Access to the inside will be very easy for both cleaning and egg collection.

CUTTING LIST AND MATERIAL REQUIREMENTS

The following list represents the cut sizes of timber required to complete the project; further cuts and alterations to individual pieces will be described in the relevant sections.

Base

- Two pieces of 50 × 25mm (2 × 1in) cut to 1.6m (63in).
- Two pieces of 50 × 25mm (2 × 1in) cut to 0.75m (29½in).
- Two 750mm lengths of 25 × 25mm (1 × 1in) cut down from a piece of 50 × 25mm (2 × 1in).

Roof and Floor

- Three pieces of 9mm (⅜in) ply cut to 0.8 × 0.8m (31½ × 31½in).
- Two 685mm (27in) lengths of 25 × 25mm (1 × 1in) cut down from a piece of 50 × 25mm (2 × 1in).

Sides

- Two triangular ends can be cut from a single piece of 9mm (⅜in) ply measuring 1.2 × 0.675m (47¼ × 26½in).

House Door

- One piece of 9mm (⅜in) ply cut to 220 × 265mm (8⅝ × 10½in).
- Two pieces of 9mm (⅜in) ply cut to 260 × 40mm (10¼ × 1½in).
- Two 260mm (10¼in) lengths of batten thinned to 12 × 25mm (½ × 1in).

Run

All components are 50 × 25mm (2 × 1in).

- Four lengths at 500mm (19¾in).
- Two lengths at 315mm (12⅜in).
- Two lengths at 800mm (31½in).
- One length at 420mm (16½in).

Run Door

- One piece of 9mm (⅜in) ply measuring 450 × 400mm (17¾ × 15¾in) – can be made from an off-cut from the end boarding.

Nest Box

- Two 100mm (4in) lengths of 25 × 25mm (1 × 1in).

- One 120mm (4¾in) length of 25 × 25mm (1 × 1in).

All other components are 9mm (⅜in) plywood.

- One piece of 420 × 265mm (16½ × 10½in).
- One piece of 325 × 100mm (12¾ × 4in).
- One piece of 300 × 120mm (11¾ × 4¾in).

Perches

- Two 770mm (30¼in) lengths of 25 × 25mm (1 × 1in). Can be thinned from 50 × 25mm (2 × 1in).
- Four 75mm (3in) lengths of 50 × 25mm (2 × 1in).

Latches

These turn-buckle devices are cut from scraps; the sizes are not crucial.

- Two 80mm (3¼in) lengths of 25 × 15mm (1 × ⅝in).
- Two 80mm (3¼in) lengths of 16 × 12mm (⅝ × ½in).

Ancillary Items

There are a number of small items that are required to complete the project. These include:

- Screws – a selection of 25mm (1in), 45mm (1¾in), ten 12mm (½in) and two 75mm (3in).
- Nails – can be used instead of screws but they do work loose over time and your project may not last as long.
- Hinges – there are five hinges in the project, some about 40mm (1½in) in length will suffice.
- Staples – galvanized wire staples are required to fit the mesh to the run.
- Tacks – 12mm (½in) steel tacks are needed to secure the roofing strip.

- Hook and eye – used to secure the opening side.
- Roof closure strip – an 800 × 100mm (31½ × 4in) strip of polythene or plastic, which can be bent over the top of the arc.
- Chicken wire or wire mesh – chicken wire is cheaper than galvanized weld mesh and is easier to work with. You will need 2m (79in) of a 0.9m (3ft) width roll for this project. If you are contemplating making a larger run or another project that requires this product, buy a big enough roll to cover all your needs.
- Wire – you will need a short (0.5m or 20in) length of wire to open and close the house door.

PREPARATION

It always helps if projects are assembled on a level surface. As with any house, we start at the bottom and work up; if the base is not square, the rest of the construction will be thrown out of kilter. After cutting all the wood, remove any rough edges and give items a light sanding if necessary.

HOW TO ASSEMBLE THE HOUSE

The Baseboard

Sort your Boards
Before you start construction of the baseboard, cast an eye over your three 0.8 × 0.8m boards and select which faces are best suited to being on show. The worst board is used for the floor.

Take one piece of 0.8 × 0.8m (31½ × 31½in) plywood and screw two 1.6m (63in) long rails of 50 × 25mm (2 × 1in) underneath it. Align the two battens underneath the plywood floor so that they are flush at one end and flush with the outer edges of the plywood. The battens are fixed with their narrowest (25mm or 1in) face against the plywood. Use 45mm (1¾in) screws driven down through the ply and into the framework. Set your screws at an equal distance apart, four each side will suffice.

The two remaining shorter 0.75m (29½in) lengths of batten can now be fixed in between the 1.6m (63in) timbers to form

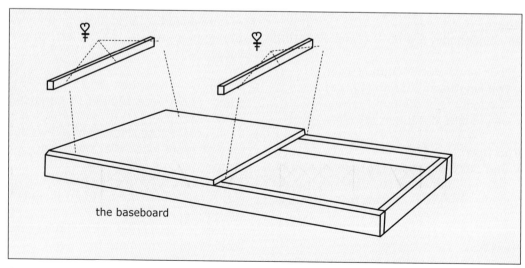

the baseboard

Construction of the house baseboard.

ends to the base unit. You are going to have to mark and pilot drill screw holes at each corner if you are to avoid splitting the wood. Use two 45mm (1¾in) screws at each joint going from the outermost side, through the long battens and into the ends of the short battens (that are fitted in between). The 0.75m (29½in) length that is situated at the end underneath the plywood floor, can also be fixed with extra screws or nails driven down through the floor into the timber below.

The baseboard requires the addition of two pieces of timber to aid the attachment of the house end panels and roof sheets. Two 750mm (29½in) lengths of 25 × 25mm (1 × 1in), cut down from a piece of 50 × 25mm (2 × 1in), are positioned across the width of the structure on the plywood floor. The pieces are situated so that they are about 25mm (1in) inwards of the edges of the floor board. The ends of these 750mm (29½in) lengths are both 25mm (1in) from their respective edges of the floor board. The pieces are fastened in place with three suitable screws in each one.

Preparation and Fitting of the Ends and Roof

The ends can both be cut from a single piece of 9mm (⅜in) ply measuring 1.2 × 0.675m (47¼ × 26½in). The required cuts are best illustrated in diagrammatic form. The formation of a doorway in one of the end pieces is a matter of both personal preference and also bird requirements. Obviously if you wish to keep Jersey Giant's, a larger hole than prescribed here will be required; nay, even a larger house! The pop hole we are advocating measures 200mm (8in) wide by 250mm (10in) high and will suit most varieties of chicken. If you wish to style an arched entrance, that is completely up to you.

The two triangular ends require some additional pieces adding to them before they are screwed in place. Two 685mm (27in) lengths of 25 × 25mm (1 × 1in) cut down from a piece of 50 × 25mm (2 × 1in) are screwed to the same inward side of both end boards. Use four 25mm (1in) screws per board. The batten is aligned so that it is flush with the sloping edge of each

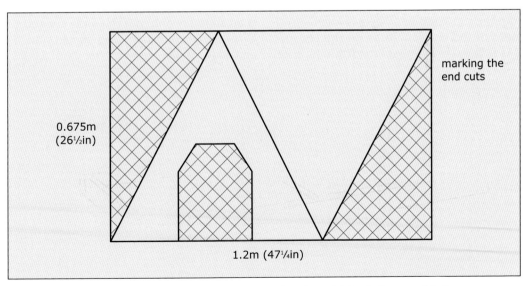

0.675m
(26½in)

marking the end cuts

1.2m (47¼in)

When marking the cuts, remember to account for the width of the saw blade.

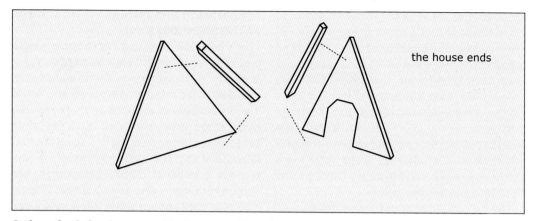

Strips of reinforcing are added to one side of the building ends.

board. The batten is positioned so that it is 30mm (1⅛in) upwards of the bottom edge of the panels.

The two 0.8 × 0.8m (31½ × 31½in) roofing sheets are joined together with three hinges along their top edge. Ensure that when the roof is in position, the best-looking sheets are facing outwards. Each hinge is fastened to the ply with 12mm (½in) screws.

The plywood ends can now be screwed to the base unit. Don't forget to position the end panel with the doorway so that it faces into the run. Each end panel is located outward of the wooden strips on the plywood base. The screws should run from the outer sides of the house, through the plywood and into the wooden floor strips. Use four screws neatly spaced along the bottom of each end.

The roof can now be placed over the upright ends of the house. Bear in mind that the roof is hinged, so there will be a fixed side and a free-moving side. You will note that we added some extra timber to the inside edges of two of the triangular ends. This was so that we could fasten the roof to these points. Ensuring that the roof is on squarely and that the ends are secure in an upright position, you should now fix one side of the roof to the end panels.

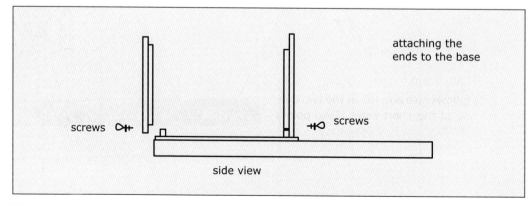

The sides are fastened on to the ends of the baseboard.

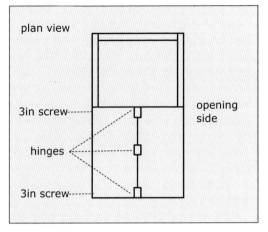

plan view

3in screw

hinges

3in screw

opening side

The sides are fastened on to the ends of the baseboard.

Screw through the roof into the purposed timbers below: four 25mm (1in) screws per edge will suffice.

It is advisable, by careful pilot drilling, to put two 75mm (3in) screws through the bottom edge of the roof (one near each corner) so that they go through the roof sheet, through the ply baseboard and into the timber bearers that are in contact with the ground.

The small gap along the top of the roof should be closed with a flexible strip of suitable heavy gauge plastic, after timber treatment has been applied.

House Door

Having opened a nice doorway, it's helpful to the hens if we find some way of filling it back in again. Take the piece of 9mm (³⁄₈in) ply cut to 220 × 265mm (8 ⅝ × 10½in) and alter it as follows: we aim to cut the two corners off one of the short sides. Take points on the edges 50mm (2in) in from both corners and cut the appropriate wedge (50mm wide by 50mm deep) off. This angled end is the top of the door. Drill a small 6mm (¼in) hole in the top edge of the door to allow an operating cord to be added later.

The next part is to add the runners that will carry the door. Hold the door in place over the door opening and mark pencil lines on the house that correspond to each edge of door. The runners need to be slightly (3mm or ¹⁄₁₆in) outward of the pencil marks to give the door a little freedom to slide. The runners are made as per the cutting list with the thinner of the pieces sandwiched between the 40mm (1½in) wide strip and the house end. It's the thinner pieces that need to be aligned with the pencil marks; the wider parts close in front of the door and prevent it from falling out. I used 45mm

Construction of the sliding door.

(1¾in) screws to fasten the runners to the house and then sawed off the metal screw protrusions on the inside.

Run

We now need to make mitre cuts to the following run components:

- Four lengths at 500mm (19¾in), we will refer to them as uprights.
- Two lengths at 315mm (12⅜in).

The cuts are at about 30 degrees but the pieces are cut slightly differently. The four 500mm lengths are all cut so that the ends slope the same way, i.e. /___ /. The two shorter lengths are cut so that the ends slope in opposing directions, i.e. /__\. All the cuts are made across the 25mm (1in) face of the components; refer to the illustrations if in doubt. One of the 315mm (12⅜in) lengths needs to be slimmed down

from 50mm (2in) to 40mm (1½in) in width.

Two of the 500mm (19¾in) uprights are positioned at the end of the run and two are positioned up against the house. The two uprights against the house will need their feet notching on the house side so that they fit flush against the house. All of the uprights slope inwards and are secured by two screws through their feet; pilot drill holes and secure with 45mm (1¾in) screws. The two uprights with notched feet can additionally be secured by screwing them to the house.

With four uprights secured in place, the two mitred 315mm (12⅜in) lengths are fixed across the tops of each pair of uprights. The slightly narrower of the two bars is fixed so that there is a gap between it and the house: this gap allows the house door to slide upwards behind it. Pilot drill holes and screw, as appropriate. The two lengths of 800mm (31½in) batten extend

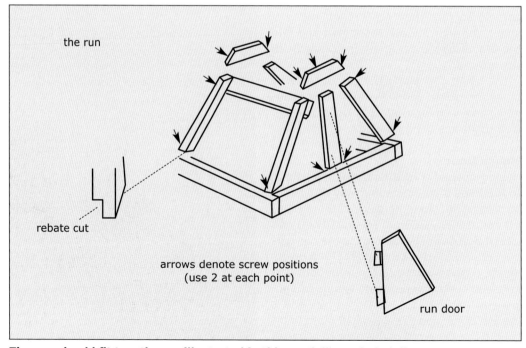

the run

rebate cut

arrows denote screw positions
(use 2 at each point)

run door

The run should fit together as illustrated in this partially exploded diagram.

the full length of the run and are fixed on the inward side of the uprights as high up as they will go. Use two screws per joint. The remaining length of 420mm (16½in) timber is a post for the run door and is fastened in a central position between the top and bottom bars at the end of the run. Use nails or screws as appropriate you will need to pilot drill and use long (75mm or 3in) fixings.

Run Door

The run door can be made from one of the 9mm (⅜in) triangular ply off-cuts left over from making the ends of the house. The door measures 450mm (17¾in) in height, 400mm (15¾in) along its bottom edge and 130mm (5⅛in) along its top edge. The door is fastened to the upright at the end of the run using two hinges. Use 25mm (1in) screws to fix the hinges to the upright and 12mm (½in) screws to fasten the hinges to the door.

Marking the Mitres

If you haven't got a protractor, hold one piece of batten flush against the slope of the roof. Mark a horizontal line across it that is parallel with the baseboard; cut along this line and you'll have a template for the correct angle.

If your run looks something like this then you're on the right lines.

The run door allows easy access for food and water.

Perches

Two 770mm (30¼in) lengths of 25 × 25mm (1 × 1in) form the perches; these can be thinned down from a piece of 50 × 25mm (2 × 1in). These are the perch bars. The perch bars are raised from floor level and sit on wooden blocks. Four 75mm (3in) lengths of 50 × 25mm (2 × 1in) make the perch supports. The supports are fitted into the house so that they sit on the wooden rails that join the house ends to the floor. The blocks stand upright and are fixed to the ends of the house using screws, fastened from the outside of the house, inwards.

Latches

These turn-buckle devices are cut from scraps; the sizes are not crucial. One latch holds the run door and another holds the side of the house shut. Take the pieces as detailed in the cutting list:

- Two 80mm (3¼in) lengths of 25 × 15mm (1 × ⅝in) are used for the house latch.
- Two 80mm (3¼in) lengths of 16 × 12mm (⅝ × ½in) are used for the run latch.

In both instances, secure one of the appropriate sized blocks to the run framework with two screws; this acts as a support for each turn-buckle. The rotating latch is fastened to the support block with one central screw. Pilot drilling of screw holes is advisory to save splitting the small wooden blocks.

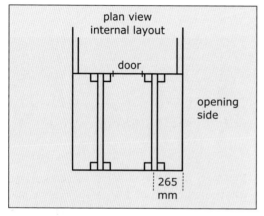

The perches rest on small blocks of wood and are positioned as illustrated in this plan view.

Wooden latches are simple to make and are used on several projects throughout the book.

This partially made divider creates an area in the house in which the birds should lay their eggs.

The house is almost complete and with divider fitted in place the finished internal layout can be seen.

Nest Box

Whilst not an absolute necessity, a nesting box is a good idea – it is a basic compartment to encourage your hens to lay in one area. A simple nest box can be made out of the off-cuts from the rest of the project.

A triangular piece of ply is used to make a component that is 420mm (16½in) high by 265mm (10½in) wide along its base. The piece has a 25mm (1in) top edge and a long sloping side of approximately 487mm (19³⁄₁₆in). One piece of 325 × 100mm (12¾ × 4in) makes a top side board for the nest and one piece of 300 × 120mm (11¾ × 4¾in) makes a bottom board. The sizes of the nest components are reliant on the nearest perch having been situated as prescribed earlier in the chapter. If you've got it wrong don't worry, unscrew the perch and reposition it.

Join the components together using the wooden blocks as corner reinforcements. Use 25mm (1in) screws for all joints. One of these blocks may need its corner

trimming slightly so that it doesn't interfere with the closure of the roof. The whole arrangement fits into the house and is screwed to the perch that has already been fitted. Two further screws are also used to secure the top board to the end wall of the chicken house.

TREATMENT

It is entirely up to the user how they wish to finish or treat their poultry house. For the sake of both finances and speed, I'd recommend any brand of fence or shed preserver. I tend to use the green stuff, it doesn't look too bad. When you paint your project, ensure that you get a good and complete covering over all the external surfaces. Work the treatment into all the exposed ends and joints. Stand the project on one end and apply a generous dose of treatment to all the areas in contact with the ground. Regular yearly top-ups of treatment will ensure that your house stays in prime condition for many years to come.

WIRE AND FIXINGS

Once the house has been painted, you can fit the plastic roof closure strip and the run covering. I used a strip of 100mm (4in) wide plastic damp-proof course but any heavy gauge polythene would do as well. Carpet tacks make ideal fixings but glue or heavy staples would do just as well.

You can either cover your run in a fine wire mesh or chicken wire. You'll need some wire cutters to cut the covering and some galvanized wire staples to fasten the covering to the framework of the run. A length of fencing wire or strong cord should be threaded through the small hole drilled in the top edge of the house door. This will enable the door to be operated from outside the run. A small screw or nail positioned on top of the run can be used to anchor the wire or cord when the door is in the open position. The last addition was an extra fastener to help secure the hinged side of the house. I used a small hook and eye at the opposite corner to where the turn-buckle is situated.

FURTHER SUGGESTIONS

With a little imagination you could do any number of things with this design. It is quite feasible to make a bigger house in length, width or depth. It would be very simple to put on a longer run; don't jump the gun, however, the next chapter will give the option of adding a large run underneath this project.

The house is finished and ready for its first inhabitants.

Chapter 2

Chicken Run

WHY BUILD A CHICKEN RUN?

The first chickens I ever bought were four retiring 72-week-old layers from a battery farm. Chickens don't generally retire at 72 weeks old but the large, intensive egg production units retire them; usually to the meat canning plant. If you're interested in the rationale behind this, it's that at about 72 weeks a bird starts to eat a little more per egg laid than it did before: a little more is not a lot with just four birds but with ten thousand the venture becomes a costly one. Still, their loss is my gain. Retiring hens are very cheap – expect to pay between fifty pence and a pound each – they soon grow new feathers and they go on laying for years. Whenever you get fresh poultry home, you will need to keep them enclosed for a period of time so that they get used to their new sleeping quarters. Whether or not you intend to keep your birds in runs, you will need a run at some stage in your poultry keeping career.

It didn't take very long from getting those first birds to wanting a lot more. Chickens come in more colours, shapes and sizes than there are days in a year; buy one and you'll want ten. The next logical progression from obtaining your first pure-bred poultry is the question of 'Do we need a cockerel?'. If you do decide to go down the route of trying to breed some pure strains of poultry, you will find that the biggest difficulty is keeping the birds segregated into their correct breeding groups; there's always some rogue cockerel who manages to get out of his proper place and mix the job up a bit.

The biggest plus point to having a run is that if you know that you will not be arriving home until after dark, you can keep your birds in the run safe in the knowledge that you won't be coming home to a garden full of feathers and blood. Visits from the fox are not only disheartening, they can be downright costly if the birds in question are expensive breeding stock.

The Chicken Run Design

In this instance we've defied general convention and gone for a chicken run that sits underneath the house. That's not to say that the run cannot be built and used as an item in its own right. This type of arrangement uses up less ground space than a house with a run at the side of it; it also has the advantage of being slightly lighter in two halves than a poultry house with a large run permanently attached.

CUTTING LIST AND MATERIAL REQUIREMENTS

The project is made from a variety of sawn lengths of 50 × 25mm (2 × 1in) treated batten.

- Four lengths of 1.5m (59in) – top and bottom lengths.
- Two lengths of 1.365m (53½in) – bottom cross-pieces (width of the run).
- Two lengths of 740mm (29⅛in) – top cross-pieces (width of the run).
- Six lengths of 710mm (28in) – diagonal uprights.
- Two lengths of 630mm (24¾in) – vertical uprights (one at each end).
- One length of 690mm (27⅛in) – top cross-member.

Ramp

- Three pieces of 9mm (⅜in) ply cut to 200 × 900mm (8 × 35½in).
- Four lengths of batten at 200mm (8in).

Ancillary Items

The run is held together with 45mm (1¾in) screws. All the holes were pilot drilled as the build progressed to avoid splitting the woodwork. The run is covered in fine chicken wire that is held to the framework with galvanized wire staples. You will need in the region of 4m² (approximately 40ft²) of chicken wire to cover the sides of the run.

You should be able to find small rolls (10m/33ft) of chicken wire in most garden centres or agricultural merchants for about ten pounds, leaving some left over for further project work.

PREPARATION

The biggest snag with building the run is that it has got to be finished so that the top is level. The upper framework of this chicken run is sized so that when the previously described project is placed on top, the woodwork of the run nestles inside the base framework of the upper building.

HOW TO ASSEMBLE THE RUN

Start by assembling a large rectangle using two lengths of 1.5m (59in) and two lengths of 1.365m (53½in). The two shorter lengths are screwed across the ends of the two longer lengths. Pilot drill your holes, go through the shorter lengths and into the ends of the 1.5m (59in) lengths.

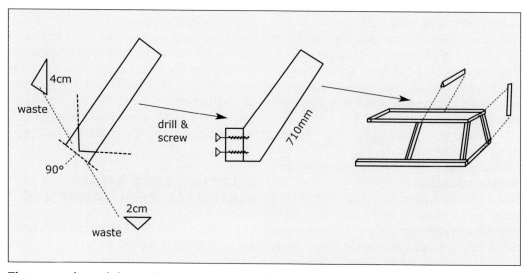

There are six uprights and they are cut and fitted as shown in the illustration.

The six 710mm (28in) diagonal uprights need to be cut to shape before they can be screwed in place. Take care to ensure that the dimensions of the six pieces are all the same prior to fixing. Uprights are fixed in each corner of the run and two are fixed at the midpoints of the run. Screws are driven

This illustrates how the uprights at the ends of the run are attached to the upper framework.

Strengthening Corners

There are two ways of improving the strength of the corners of 90-degree butt joints, such as used here. You can use commercially available steel corner braces, the smallest of which are only about ten pence each. Small triangles of plywood fixed across corners are another great way of improving joint strength as we shall use later in the book.

The overall construction of the run and the positions of individual components can be seen in this picture.

If you've cut your uprights correctly, the finished joints should look like this.

floor area rectangle. The middle timbers are only secured with two screws each. The corner uprights can be secured with screws from both directions so that four screws are holding them in place.

The upper framework comprising two lengths of 1.5m (59in) and two lengths of 740mm (29⅛in) can be made in the same fashion as the previous rectangle. Once this has been fastened together, it can be carefully positioned over the top of the uprights. Screw the top framework to the uprights. The middle joints are secured with one screw per side angled slightly downwards (rather than horizontally).

There is a 690mm (27⅛in) length of batten referred to as the top cross-member in the cutting list. This piece is fastened between the two sides in the central top portion of the run. The bar is located

through the lower framework (from the outside) and into the upright timbers that are positioned on the inward side of the

The ramp. Note the position of the wooden block underneath the ramp. The top end of the ramp is secured to the bar above it.

adjacent to where the uprights join the top framework. Secure this piece with two screws per end.

There are two additional timbers that need adding, one at either end of the run. These are positioned as vertical bracing at each end of the run. The timbers are located on the inward side of the run in a measured central position. They are secured top and bottom with two screws per joint.

Ramp

In order for the proposed chickens in the run to be able to access their house, they will need a ramp. The ramp is a simple affair constructed from a length of ply with some pieces of batten screwed to it at regular intervals to act as rungs. I've spaced my battens at 150mm (6in), which means that if you start with a gap before the first attachment point, four rungs will be enough to span the length of the board.

The ramp is fitted centrally between the bar that runs across the top of the run and the lower timber work at the end of the run. The top end of the ramp is screwed to the underside of the cross bar. The bottom end of the ramp is fastened to a small block of wood (approximately 50 × 50mm (2 × 2in), which is screwed to the timber work at the end of the run, this raises the end of the ramp up slightly from floor level.

TREATMENT WIRE AND FIXINGS

Despite the fact that the roofing battens I use for these projects are tanalised, I still tend to paint or treat them for both cosmetic and longevity purposes. I have used chicken net to cover my run. For the sake of making life easy, cover the sides and ends of the run as separate entities rather

The run is finished and has been covered in wire. You could cover the run, remove the ramp and use it with any other poultry house.

than trying to wrap wire around the edges and corners. Try and achieve some degree of tension in the netting so that you aren't left with 'sagging' and 'gathers' in the wire net.

FURTHER SUGGESTIONS

Alterations
The basic design of the run can be altered to use as a stand-alone device for anything else, it might do a rabbit or a guinea pig. Firstly you won't need the ramp if it's going to be used without the previous chapter's project. If you are intending to use the run with a different style of chicken house, it's a simple enough job to wire up the top opening and make a bespoke opening or add a plywood door in one of the sides.

Breeding Chickens
If you do decide to have a go at breeding chickens, a good book on the subject will go a long way to help you get started. Birds are generally kept in accommodation, such as this, in breeding trio's (two hens and a cock). People breed birds for egg-laying, for meat, for showing, for breed improvement, for financial reward or simply for pleasure. Buying the best stock you can afford from a reputable breeder is the best way of ensuring that your hobby will get off to the best possible start. Please don't think there is a fast buck to be made, there isn't – I've tried it! If you start with decent poultry, aside from egg production, you do at least have the chance of producing some

The house from the previous project has been designed to fit snugly on top of the run.

well-bred progeny that someone may want to buy. Start with rubbish and you could well end up overrun with young stock that nobody wants. The point behind breeding chickens on a small scale, as I have always seen it, is to produce a modest surplus of fresh eggs at no cost with the added bonus of the occasional chickens to sell or fat cockerel to eat. Certainly not get rich quick but by no means running at a loss.

Chapter 3

Dog Kennel

FIRST GET A DOG

My first and only dog to date is a Border Collie named Moss. He started as Moss or Mossy but has now evolved to Mr Mostyn Dog. Collies are highly intelligent and have excellent temperaments if they are kept busy. Let them get bored, however, and they will degenerate into some of the worst dogs alive. A Collie is definitely not a dog for the back garden; they want to work hard (most of the time) and are affectionate and loyal. Whilst we are not advocating that the readership should go Collie shopping, one of the plus points is that these dogs don't mind living outside in all weathers – ours gets positively fed up when he's kept inside. This trait is especially useful if he's been eating sheep muck and you'd prefer to keep him at arm's length.

We've been through a series of incarnations of dog houses for Moss dog; this is the latest design, although whether or not he'll take ownership of it remains to be debated. When designing wooden housing one must remember that first and foremost, the object must be relatively easy to make. As a farmer, writer and dreamer-up-of-ideas, it's no good cooking up convoluted or intricate designs if people soon lose interest and can't follow them. Coupled with ease of manufacture is cost; thankfully there is some happy ground between being overly cheap and cheerful, and looking good for a minimal cost. This project tends towards the latter. This kennel design could be scaled up or down and, as illustrated and described, will fit any medium-sized hound – I'd class a Collie or a Labrador as such. If you have a St Bernard, it's obviously going to cost a fair bit extra to build the kennel.

CUTTING LIST AND MATERIAL REQUIREMENTS

The kennel is constructed from 9mm (³⁄₈in) plywood; 50 × 25mm (2 × 1in) battening is used for structural bracing and some pieces of 75 × 50mm (3 × 2in) are used to support the floor.

Base
- One piece of 9mm (³⁄₈in) ply cut to 1.0 × 0.6m (39³⁄₈ × 23⁵⁄₈in).
- Threes pieces of 75 × 50mm (3 × 2in) cut to 0.6m (23⁵⁄₈in) length.

Sides
- Two pieces of 9mm (³⁄₈in) ply cut to 1.0 × 0.5m (39³⁄₈ × 19⁵⁄₈in).

Ends
The ends are altered from two pieces of 9mm (³⁄₈in) ply cut to 0.8 × 0.62m (31¹⁄₂ × 24³⁄₈in).

The following pieces of 50 × 25mm (2 × 1in) batten are required:

■ Four lengths of 350mm (13¾in).
■ Four lengths of 450mm (17¾in).

Roof

The roof is made from two sheets of ply both measuring 1.04 × 0.45m (41 × 17¾in).

A roof support is made from 1m (39⅜in) of 50 × 25mm (2 × 1in) batten.

Flash Band

Builder's flash band is used for sealing and repairing cracks in roofs and masonry. It comes in a roll in widths of 15cm (6in) plus. On the exterior side, it has a metallic finish giving the appearance of traditional lead flashing. On the inward side, a bituminous coating allows the 'tape' to adhere to a wide variety of surfaces including wood and masonry. It is inexpensive and is an ideal companion in the construction of waterproof animal housing.

Ancillary Items

A selection of suitable length screws or nails is required; I'd recommend 30mm (1¼in) as adequate. The roof-closure strip was made from a piece of builder's flash band. If this is not available, a strip of plastic, roofing felt or other similar material could be used instead.

PREPARATION

As the finished article is relatively large, make sure you are assembling it on a level surface with sufficient working room around it. It may be worth mentioning that you should ensure that you can get both this and the other projects out through the door when you have finished building them!

HOW TO ASSEMBLE THE HOUSE

The project is not at all difficult to assemble and once the components have been cut to size, the kennel should very soon start to take shape.

The Baseboard

Start by assembling the base of the kennel. Position the three pieces of 75 × 50mm (3 × 2in) underneath the piece of 9mm (⅜in) ply. Remember the base board is the plywood piece measuring 1 × 0.6m (39¾ × 23⅝in). The timbers are positioned, one under each side and one in the middle; the 75mm (3in) surfaces of the support timbers are in contact with the ply floor. Drive nails or screws down through the plywood and into the supports underneath. Use at least three fixings per timber.

Preparation and Fitting of the Ends

One of the pieces of plywood earmarked for the kennel ends (two ply pieces measuring 0.8 × 0.62m (31½ × 24⅜in)) needs to have a dog doorway marked and cut in it. Both the end panels also need an apex cutting to carry the roof. In order to mark the doorway you will need a set of compasses (as used at school), or a drawing pin, a piece of string and a pencil can suffice just as well. Use an electric reciprocating saw (jigsaw) to make the curved doorway cuts. If you do not have such a saw, you could still

---

Marking a Curve

Tie a length of string to a pencil. Tie the knot as close to the pencil point as it will go without slipping off. Put a drawing pin through the string at a length that corresponds to the radius of the curve – in this instance 175mm (7in). Position the drawing pin at the centre point of the proposed imaginary circle. Keeping the string taut, draw your curve.

Start by making up the floor

remove the required material with a normal panel saw and a coping saw to help around the edges. I will add at this point that the size and shape of your doorway is a matter of personal preference. If you have a large dog, you could make the doorway bigger and vice versa.

Once the panels are cut as required, they need some bracing adding to them on the inward facing side. Use the four lengths of 450mm (17¾in) batten as uprights. Mount them 10mm (⅜in) inward of the vertical edge of each end section. The bottom of each batten length is not flush with the bottom of each end panel. These lengths are mounted 40mm (1½in) inboard of the bottom of each panel. The battens are secured to the plywood using three screws per piece. Screw through the ply and into the battening. The shorter 350mm (13¾in)

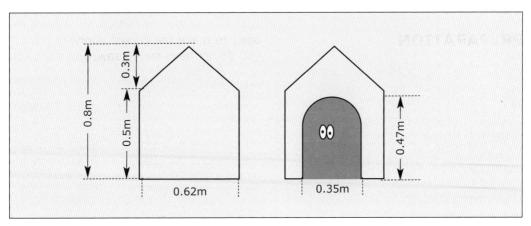

Mark and cut the side panels as illustrated.

Make up the side panels, positioning the reinforcing timber as shown here.

The side panels will sit on the baseboard and the fixings are driven into the timber underneath.

lengths of batten are used to reinforce the end panels along their apexes. This in turn will give something substantial to screw the roof to. (The apex is the part of the end of the kennel shaped like an A that supports the roof.)

It's now time to fix the end panels to the baseboard. It should be evident that with the battening added to the plywood ends, the side panels should sit on the baseboard. The bracing batten will sit on the baseboard with the plywood protruding downwards over the blocks of wood under the base. Nail (or screw) the end panels through the plywood and into the blocks of wood underneath the kennel. Use three or four fixings per side.

Adding the Side Panels

With the kennel ends in place, it is now evident that you can align and screw the plywood sides straight on to the wooden battening that is attached to the end panels. Align the top and bottom edges of the side panels with the two ends, prior to permanent fixing. Use four screws per joint. We can also add three extra fastenings along the bottom edges of each side. Drive a fixing through the plywood and into the end of each of the support blocks that are underneath the kennel floor.

Adding the Roof

If you've worked through your cutting list correctly, there should only be three pieces of timber left: two roofing sheets and a length of batten. Screw the length of batten between the apexes of the two end panels as a sort of ridge bar. You can now position your roofing sheets against this bar. Fix each sheet in place using screws into the woodwork of each end panel and also into the ridge bar. In the design I neglected to add extra timber that would allow the lower edges of the roof to be joined to the sides of the kennel. You could add a

length of batten along the top edges of each side, if you require, before the roof is fixed on. The design is still sturdy without this addition.

There will by design be a slight overlap of the roofing sheets at each end of the kennel. The roof is finished off with a closure strip to prevent water getting in through the ridge. If you don't have any flash band, you could use a strip of flexible heavy gauge polythene or plastic. Failing that, polyurethane wood glue or wood filler could be used to plug the seam. You could do away with a roof closure strip altogether if you are intending to cover the roof. I intend to paint my roof with a covering of Ronseal, which dries into an almost plastic-like coating that is impervious to water. In projects past, I have successfully covered buildings with roofing felt, heavy gauge polythene and even feather-edge boarding for a really

As well as fastening on the side panels, a ridge bar is added to support the roof.

fancy finish. If using bitumen felt, plastic sheet or other waterproof fabric, you will need to use felt nails (the stubby galvanized one's with the large heads). The lower edges of any roof covering you decide to use are best secured strips of batten along the lower edges of the roof. Otherwise what tends to happen is the wind gets under the felt and rips it of. Take it from experience!

The lower edges of any roof covering you decide to use are best secured by fixing strips of batten along the lower edges of the roof. This will help keep the covering on the roof in windy weather.

TREATMENT

Work plenty of paint or treatment into the corners and seams if you want to avoid your plywood de-laminating. Also remember to give the blocks underneath the kennel a thorough coating, as these will be in contact with the ground and will otherwise rot over time. Don't forget that a dog will often chew the area around the entrance, so don't use anything too noxious for a coating.

FURTHER SUGGESTIONS

What we have attempted to design and build is a basic easy-to-manufacture dog kennel. If your dog is a King Charles Spaniel and requires something a little more upmarket, you could either add some manufactured architrave under the eaves and gable ends of the roof, or you could cut some out of some of your plywood off-cuts. If your mutt sleeps outside, don't face the kennel into the prevailing win – you probably wouldn't want to sleep in a permanent draught either. You could line the kennel floor with a bit of old rug or carpet; blankets do just as well but they do need cleaning or replacing occasionally.

With the addition of the roof panels and a closure strip, the kennel is finished.

Of course every finished product needs a qualified inspector.

Chapter 4

Bantam Chicken House

AN INTRODUCTION TO BANTAM CHICKENS

Many of the breeds and variations of chicken that we have today have a Bantam or miniature equivalent. There are also varieties of small chickens that do not have a large equivalent; these are referred to as True Bantams. Bantam breeds are about a quarter of the size of their regular counterparts in terms of body mass; not much of a dinner you might say. Such is the following of Bantam breeds that aficionados often remain with the Bantam breeds, ignoring their larger counterparts. It is true that Bantam poultry are certainly intriguing; the hens will certainly hold their own against the larger varieties in mixed flocks. Many a Bantam cock suffers from the delusion that he can punch as hard as a fully grown chicken; some of them actually do.

There are advantages to keeping Bantams, the main ones being as follows:

- they eat less;
- they are less destructive when free-ranging;
- they don't require as much room when kept in confined runs;
- they are exceptionally good mothers and can be used to incubate other eggs (including goose eggs!).

Obviously, the down side of being so small is that the chicken doesn't lay such a large egg. That's certainly not to deride the Bantam breeds for their egg-laying ability; it's just the egg is smaller. If you want to breed birds for the table, Bantams are of little use to you. Traditionally, the Gypsy communities have always been big on Bantams; many traditional bow-top caravans have a small chicken crate or house at the rear; they are an easy bird to move about. I have been asked (even recently) by the local travelling gate salesman for Bantam eggs over normal varieties. An expert might say they actually taste different, I'm not so sure, probably only because I have the palette and taste buds of a philistine.

Building Your Own Bantie House

It doesn't take a great deal in the way of materials to build a house with an occasional run for a trio of bantam chickens. I try and produce chicken housing designs with a small run so that chickens can be left with food and water for a day or so in the

---

Broodiness
Broodiness is the term by which a chicken's ability to sit on eggs is loosely measured. Modern hybrid layers have all but had it bred out of them; you'll only get the odd one go broody in a large flock. Some bantams will do little else but sit on eggs over the summer, rearing two or even three broods in a year.

average garden. Left to their own free-ranging devices, chickens are extremely damaging to borders and vegetable gardens. If you are new to poultry, I'd again advise you not to leave your poultry unattended. You have been warned!

The Chicken House Design

None of these designs requires any complicated woodworking techniques. With this project you could just leave it as a small stand-alone house, if wanted. The house is of a lean-to design opening into a small run. As the house is relatively small, the roof simply lifts off; when the house needs cleaning, the main detritus can be lifted out and the floor of the house swept out through the doorway.

CUTTING LIST AND MATERIAL REQUIREMENTS

Base

- One piece of 9mm (⅜in) ply measuring 400 × 500mm (15¾ × 19⅝in).

The following pieces of 50 × 25mm (2 × 1in) batten are required:

- Two lengths of 500mm (19⅝in).
- Two lengths of 350mm (13¾in).

Sides

To be cut from two pieces of 9mm (⅜in) ply measuring 400 × 500mm (15¾ × 19⅝in).

The following pieces of 50 × 25mm (2 × 1in) batten are required:

- Two lengths of 375mm (14¾in).
- Two lengths of 325mm (12¾in).

Front and Back

- One piece of 9mm (⅜in) ply measuring 400 × 420mm (15¾ × 16½in).

- One piece of 9mm (⅜in) ply measuring 350 × 420mm (13¾ × 16½in).
- One piece of 9mm (⅜in) ply measuring 160 × 200mm (6¼ × 7⅞in).

Roof

- One piece of 9mm (⅜in) ply measuring 535 × 450mm (21 × 17¾in).
- Two lengths of 50 × 25mm (2 × 1in) batten cut to 400mm (15¾in).

Run

The following pieces of 50 × 25mm (2 × 1in) batten are required:

- Four lengths of 1.5m (59in).
- Two lengths of 380mm (15in).
- Three lengths of 420mm (16½in).

Run Door

- One piece of 9mm (⅜in) ply measuring 470 × 360mm (18½ × 14⅛in).

Ancillary Items

To cover the run you will need a quantity of weld mesh or chicken netting (between 1.5 and 2m² (15–20ft²) and sufficient wire staples to attach the covering to the framework. Four small hinges are needed: a pair for the house door and a pair for the run door. A hook and eye is required for the run door and a couple for the roof. A single screw-in eye is required for the house door; this will allow the addition of a length of wire or cord by which the door can be operated externally from the run. A selection of 30mm (1¼in) screws or nails are required to make the house and some 40–45mm (1¾in) screws are needed to make up the run. Small 12mm (½in) screws are used wherever hinges are attached to plywood (twelve needed in total).

HOW TO ASSEMBLE THE HOUSE

The Baseboard

As always, start by assembling the base. Take the 400 × 500mm (15¾ × 19⅝in) piece of ply and arrange the corresponding battening (from the cutting list) around the edge. It's the narrowest (25mm or 1in) surface of the batten that's in contact with the plywood. Drive screws or nails through the plywood and down into the rectangle of timber work below.

> **Spacing of Screws and Nails**
> Unless otherwise stated, space screws and nails at even intervals along a join. A gap of about 150mm (6in) between each fixing won't leave you wrong.

Preparation and Fitting of the Sides

The side panels both need a 50mm (2in) deep wedge cutting from their longest edges. The side panels both measure 400 × 500mm (15¾ × 19⅝in); the longest edges will be fixed to the base. Mark a point 50mm (2in) down one of the 400mm (15¾in) sides and join this point to the opposite top corner to remove the required small wedge. This will create the lean-to style roof. One of the edges of each panel will now measure 350mm (13¾in) instead of 400mm (15¾in).

Take each of the side panels and the corresponding lengths of batten from the cutting list. Remember that the top edge of each panel is the sloping one. Position the battens so that they touch the side edge and top edge of each panel, you will note that the battens do not extend all the way to the bottom of the sheet. The 375mm (14¾in) lengths are fastened to the 400mm (15¾in) edges and the 325mm (12¾in) lengths are fixed to the 350mm (13¾in) edges. Remember that you are making up two panels that sit opposite each other on the base. The panels are symmetrical, not identical. When making up the second panel, take care that your strips of wood are added to the correct side of the sheet. If you hold the two panels together, all the extra added timbers should be sandwiched in between the two sheets.

A side panel is fitted in place on the baseboard.

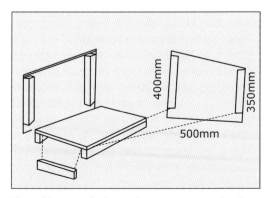

The side panels have been cut to a sloping profile.

The sides are in place and the door panel is added.

The side panels can now be fixed into position on the base board. Place each panel in position against the base and drive fixings (nails or screws) through the skirt of overlapping plywood at the bottom of each sheet.

Preparation and Fitting of the Front and Back

The back panel measures 350 × 420mm (13¾in × 16½in) and can be aligned and fastened in place without any further modification. Use three screws per corner. The front panel measures 400 × 420mm (15¾in × 16½in) and requires the addition of a doorway prior to fitting. I've designed the doorway to measure 140mm (5½in) wide by 180mm (7in) high, as this will accommodate the Light Sussex Bantam chickens that I own. The door can be cut out using an electric jigsaw. You can opt for a rounded doorway or square if you so desire. After the doorway has been cut out, the finished panel can be screwed in place using four 30mm (1¼in) screws per corner.

There is little use having the doorway without a door, which is a piece of plywood measuring 160 × 200mm (6¼ × 7⅞in). Add two hinges to one of the shorter edges of the door. Use short screws 12mm (½in) to attach the hinges to the plywood. I've hinged my door at the bottom edge and intend to add a screw-in eye to which I can attach a wire or a cord. This feature will enable the user to close the door from outside the run.

Add the rear panel and then add a ramp.

The roof panel fits into the top of the house; provided that you fix the two strips of timber in the correct place. The two strips are shown as lighter-coloured timber in this photograph.

The Roof

The roof needs the addition of two lengths of batten, which are set 25mm (1in) inward from each of the longest sides. The two battens are positioned equidistantly, leaving a gap of approximately 65mm (2½in) between the batten ends and the edges of the roof.

Providing the lengths of timber have been fixed in the correct position, the roof should fit into the top of the building. With the roof in place, a hook and eye set can be added to each side of the house to hold the roof on during windy weather. With the roof in position, screw in two eyes to the underside of the roof about halfway along each side. Add the hooks as appropriate so that they engage with the eyes. The hooks are screwed into the sides of the house.

The finished house. It could be used as a stand-alone item for a trio of bantam chickens.

Run

The addition of the run greatly improves a very basic house design. Working on a level surface, use 45mm (1¾in) screws to secure a 1.5m (59in) length of batten to each side of the house at floor level. These two pieces of batten run down the length of the house protruding about a 1m (3.3ft), which will be the area encompassed by the run. With these first two bars in place, screw a length of 420mm (16½in) batten between the outward ends of the two protruding timbers.

The next additions are two uprights at the end of the run. Use the two pieces of 380mm (15in) material in each of the two corners of the ground-level frame; screw them in place. You'd be well advised to use screws for all joints in this run construction project. Screws will produce a sturdier finish than nails.

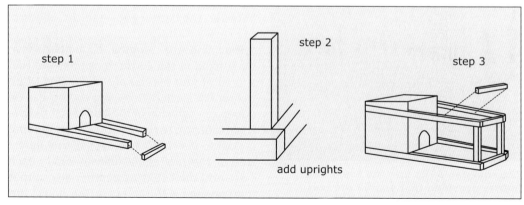

The run is made up in steps as illustrated here. A full description of construction is outlined in the text.

The make-up of the joints is shown. Note the screw positions.

The opening on top of the run has been designed to allow access for food and water.

Add the two upper timbers 1.5m (59in) of the run. These are the same size as the previously positioned lower timbers. You should be able to align the upper bars so that they run parallel with the lower framework. When securing these bars to the

The woodwork is almost finished and only treatment and covering remain.

Woodworking Tip

In most occasions, I've neglected to drill pilot holes prior to screwing timbers together. If you are making a joint close to the edge or end of a piece of wood, drilling a pilot hole is advisable as it prevents splitting the grain apart when the screw is driven in. To make these pilot holes, use a drill that is slightly smaller than the screw diameter.

house, use shorter screws. You should fix the top bars of the run in place by driving screws through from the inside of the house. You can also add another length of 420mm (16½in) cross piece between the open ends of these two top bars. What remains is to secure these two long top bars to the pieces of vertical batten that are at the end of the run. Observe the illustrations and use screws as required.

Run Door

A piece of 9mm (⅜in) ply measuring 470 × 360mm (18½ × 14⅛in) is used for the run door. This enables us to have some means of putting food and water into the chicken run. The door is hinged with two 40mm (1½in) hinges. The hinges are fastened to the plywood with 12mm (½in) screws. The run needs an extra bar adding into the top of it; this will give us something that the door and its hinges can be attached to. Add the remaining piece of 420mm (16½in) batten (from the cutting list) into the top of the run. This bar will be situated about 380mm (15in) from the end of the run but you should check the position prior to fixing by putting the door into position on top of the run and seeing where the hinges lie. The run door can be fastened with the addition of a hook and eye on the side.

The run door is added.

The run is complete. I'll probably use it for growing chicks next year.

Perches

I neglected to add perches in my prototype design, but it's an easy enough task to measure the inside width of the house, cut some batten down to 12 × 12mm (1 × 1in) and to the required length. Perches can be secured in place by screwing through the walls of the house and into the ends of the perching bars.

TREATMENT

The best stuff for treating poultry houses is the inexpensive green-coloured shed and fence preserver that can be bought in budget and DIY shops around our Fair Isle. Remember that with poultry runs, there is a fair bit of timber in contact with the ground, so they do need a liberal coating of preserver if they are to last. Using tanalised (heat and pressure treated) timber helps a lot. Paint the project prior to the addition of the wire covering, not after; the recommended way does make the job a fair bit easier.

WIRE AND FIXINGS

I used fine chicken netting for the covering of my run. It's inexpensive and relatively easy to cut and work with. Fasten the netting to the timbers of the run with wire staples – the type that look like the letter U. I have tried using a commercial upholsterer's staple gun, which does work although I doubt that the longevity of fine wire staples is up to much.

Working with Chicken Wire

When you cut chicken wire it tends to leave lots of spiky little points that you can catch your hands and clothes on. There are three ways of dealing with this:

- Firstly, cover all the exposed edges in a second layer of thinner, cosmetic timber.
- Secondly, use some fine cutters to remove most of the sharp points.
- Thirdly, and possibly the easiest method, is to fold the edge so that the points are folded over and facing into the timber rather than outwards. Trap this folded edge between the timber and the better side of wire.

Grit

Chickens need grit (very small stones) as part of their diet. It aids the digestion process of the bird by helping to break up food in the gizzard. Free-range chickens will naturally have access to plenty of grit; confined birds do not. Commercially available layers pellets will contain a balanced diet for the egg-laying bird but they are not a stand-alone tonic when it comes to general avian health.

FURTHER SUGGESTIONS

This was intended to be a small, easy-to-make project to help keep Bantam chickens. If you prefer this type of chicken house design to the previous one, you could always scale up the project into something that would better accommodate larger breeds. If you decide to build a bigger run, it is often a great idea to add some wheels on one end and some handles on the other, so that you can move it around on your own.

Remember that if you do keep chickens in a run, you need to move the run regularly to a new patch of ground. It is worth considering that, as well as gaining vital grit and nutrients from the grass and soil, chickens do excrete droppings that contain parasites. There is a common misconception that a chicken can be kept in a run and fed household scraps and it will keep laying lots of eggs: it will not. That's not to say that chickens won't eat vegetable peelings or bread off-cuts but they do need large quantities of calcium to keep forming egg shells day after day. A second-hand battery hen will produce five to six eggs a week for forty or more weeks of the year, if it is fed correctly. Free-ranging birds will find a comprise between egg quantity and what nutrition they can find locally. Enclosed birds will stop laying if their diet is lacking in the nutritional elements that they require.

Moving your chicken run on a regular basis will help curtail the build up of parasitic worms that detract from the health and well-being of your birds.

Chickens do need periodic worming, regardless of whether they are kept free-range or confined. There are some naturally based products that are available, although I'm not sure of their efficacy. The most widely known commercial wormer is known as Flubenvet, which is what most of the breeders and farmers that I know are given to using. Whether or not you keep chickens for eggs or breeding purposes it is a given that they need to be kept in good health. Regular rotation of ground coupled with a correct diet and a regular worming regime will give you healthy happy laying birds for years to come.

Chapter 5

Dovecote

HISTORY AND USAGE

It is said that the ancient Egyptians kept domesticated doves or at least something pretty close. It would appear that dove and pigeon keeping was certainly in common practice in the Eastern countries many centuries prior to its introduction to Europe. With the constant expeditionary warfare of the Middle Ages, including the Crusades, came the spread of ideas. With the spread of new knowledge arguably came the spread of domesticated dove and pigeon droppings. The Normans were the first big bird fanciers in this land who also incorporated bird lofts into their castle designs. So dovecotes can unequivocally be blamed on William the Conqueror. It is at this point that you are probably wondering what on earth people wanted the doves for anyway – it certainly wouldn't have been pet value. Both doves and pigeons rapidly reproduce and so meat, eggs, feathers and bird muck were never in short supply. Whilst it's obvious what the first three products could be used for, it is worth stating that the nitrogen content of this type of bird muck is very high and so it made excellent fertilizer for the fields and vegetable gardens of the day.

I'm not sure at what point dovecotes really started drifting out of vogue; certainly, the early 1900s would probably be a good period from which to start charting their demise. We recently moved from a moorland farm that would have been built in the 1800s. Several of the buildings of this establishment, including the main house, had pigeon lofts or dovecotes incorporated in the roof. The largest loft in the main barn was still in use with a permanent population of filthy pigeons; it's a pity no-one still bothered to eat some of them.

And on to the present era. There are still many historical dovecotes dotted about our landscape, although these days the most obvious examples are the wooden and free-standing structures such as we are about to build. Wooden dovecotes are often mounted on poles and are square, hexagonal or even octagonal in shape. For the sake of simplicity we are going to build a square dovecote with four separate compartments.

You can buy beautiful ornamental doves and pigeons from many poultry auctions and sales. This project can be mounted on a pole in your garden yard or driveway and will serve as an excellent ornamental feature and point of interest. Just be sure to mount it out of the reach of cats.

The Dovecote Design

The design is square with a pointed roof. It is all made from readily available plywood and timber. Plenty of screws are required but no hinges or other ironmongery. There are two separate floors in the house, each with a small alighting board. Each floor is divided into two sections, so that the house has separate entrances to the four different compartments.

CUTTING LIST AND MATERIAL REQUIREMENTS

Floors
- Two pieces of 9mm (³⁄₈in) ply cut to 480 × 480mm (19 × 19in).

The following pieces of 50 × 25mm (2 × 1in) batten are required:

- Four pieces of 480mm (18⁷⁄₈in).
- Four pieces of 160mm (6¼in).

Roof
- Four pieces will be cut from one piece of 9mm (³⁄₈in) ply cut to 1400 × 500mm (55 × 19⁵⁄₈in).

Sides
- Two pieces of 9mm (³⁄₈in) ply cut to 500 × 500mm (19⁵⁄₈ × 19⁵⁄₈in).
- Two pieces of 9mm (³⁄₈in) ply cut to 500 × 480mm (19⁵⁄₈ × 18⁷⁄₈in).

The following pieces of 50 × 25mm (2 × 1in) batten are required:

- Two pieces of 480mm (18⁷⁄₈in).
- Two pieces of 430mm (16¹⁵⁄₁₆in).

Partitions
- Two pieces of 9mm (³⁄₈in) ply cut to 230 × 670mm (9 × 26³⁄₈in).

Perches
- Four off-cuts of batten cut to 100mm (4in).

Bracket and Pole
The following items can be made from either of the standard dimensions of timber. I used the heavier gauge but the lighter would have sufficed:

- One piece of 75 × 50mm (3 × 2in) or 100 × 50mm (4 × 2in) cut to 450mm (17¾in).

- Two pieces of 75 × 50mm (3 × 2in) or 100 × 50mm (4 × 2in) cut to 280mm (11in).
- One piece of 75 × 50mm (3 × 2in) or 100 × 50mm (4 × 2in) cut to required height for a pole – I'd suggest about 2m (6ft 7in).

Ancillary Items
In retrospect I would say that the project needs the addition of some polyurethane wood glue and some panel pins. The joins on the roof have been finished off with some 5cm (2in) wide strips of builder's flash band. If your roof joins don't end up as close as you would like, you have the option of using wood filler on the seams. If you are not happy with that, you can always make up some strips of roofing shingles (tiles) out of bitumen roofing felt. Cut the felt into strips and turn it into a UUUU pattern. When glued or fixed in place, these sections can be used to produce an attractive finish. Four 6 × 80mm (¼ × 3in) coach bolts are required to clamp the house to the stand.

HOW TO ASSEMBLE THE HOUSE

The Baseboards
For the main board that will form the base of the project, use one of the pieces of 9mm (³⁄₈in) ply as the floor board and fix

Tool Tips
My favourite tool is called a Yankee Screwdriver, manufactured by Stanley. It is one of those that, as you push the handle in, the tool bit rotates. I've driven thousands of screws with it and never once did it need re-charging. The point is, it doesn't need re-charging; it takes very little effort to operate. I just can't stand cordless devices that constantly need to be on the charger.

The upper floor is on the left. The right-hand panel is the underside of the dovecote. The additional wood was an abortive attempt at a support bracket that wasn't strong enough.

lengths of 50 × 25mm (2 × 1in) batten around the edge as described and illustrated. Use two lengths of 480mm (18⅞in), batten on opposite sides of the board. Use

The lower-level baseboard. The two openings correspond with the doors in the panels.

the smaller pieces of 160mm (6¼in) batten, two along each remaining edge, leaving a gap for the doorway in the centre portion of each side.

The second baseboard is a far simpler affair and only requires the addition of two 480mm (18⅞in) lengths of batten down the edges of the opposite sides.

Preparation and Fitting of the Sides

Prior to fitting the sides to the baseboards, doorways need cutting in all of the four sides. Two of the sides will have a doorway at the bottom and the other two sides will have a door cut halfway up. Don't forget that the four sides are not the same size. Cut the bottom doorways in a central position in the two 480mm (19⅝in) sides, and central doorways in the other two matching sides. The two upper doorways are positioned in the centre of each 500 × 500mm (19⅝in × 19⅝in) sheet. The distance between the bottom of the doorway and the bottom of the sheet is 250mm (10in). The doorways are 100mm (4in) wide and

120mm (4¾in) high at their full extent. All the doorways have an arched profile. Mark the doors and cut out using a jigsaw. To start the cuts on the doors that are in the middle of the sheets, use an electric drill to drill a hole that's big enough to get your saw blade into. When you have finished the cutting out, give the edges of the doorway a light sanding. Prior to attaching the sides to the bases, add the small perches to the two sides that have an upper doorway. The perches are only small off-cuts of batten and are screwed to the plywood so as to be level with the bottom of each doorway.

Select one of the baseboards and orientate it so that the battens are facing upwards. Start attaching the sides using 30mm (1¼in) screws. Use four screws per side. Start by fixing the two 500 × 480mm (19⅝x 18⅞in) sides opposite each other. Add the two 500 × 500mm (19⅝x 19⅝in)

sides so that all the four corners are flush and square.

The remaining two perches can be added. These two lower perches are set back 12mm (½in) underneath each of the doorways. They are secured by two screws each, driven through the floor close to the edge of each entrance.

Before further assembly, we need to make provision for attaching the structure to a pole. Sit the project on top of the 450mm (17¾in) piece of 75 × 50mm (3 × 2in) or 100 × 50mm (4 × 2in) Orientate the piece of wood so that it is both central and running between the two lower doorways. Drill holes down through the floor of the house and through the heavy timber underneath. Drill two holes spaced about 40mm (1½in) apart just inside each doorway. Drill the holes far enough from the door that they are fairly well set back from the ends

Two pairs of side panels are made as illustrated. Perch blocks are shown on the upper doorway.

Prior to adding the middle floor, a partition is put in the house.

of the heavy sub-floor timber. Later on when the house is complete, you should be able to put your hand through each doorway and put bolts into their respective holes, which will fix the house to the stand.

Partitions

Partitions are used to divide each floor area into two separate nesting spaces. Before the upper floor is fixed in place, a partition is needed on the lower level. For the sake of simplicity I have put a partition diagonally across the lower floor. The reality is that this type of partition just slots in and doesn't need any fixing in place. Because of the internal battening at floor level, the lower partition requires a small square (approximately 50 × 50mm or 2 × 2in) to be removed from each of the bottom corners of the partition board. The upper partition requires similar 25 × 50mm (1 × 2in) corners removing from its lower edge.

The middle floor can be placed into the dovecote, again with the battening facing upward. The reinforced edges of the middle

The middle floor sits on top of the partition and is fixed in place. Internal edging has been applied to the top of the house.

floor give us some substantial timber that can be used to hold the entire dovecote structure together. Try and keep the floor level as you drive screws through the wall of the dovecote and into the battening that is attached to the upper floor. Use three or four screws per side, ensuring that all the screws are positioned so as to catch the batten on the inside of the dovecote.

The next partition can now be put into place. To be honest, I'm not sure whether or not the birds might vaguely object to living in the triangular-shaped rooms on the lower deck. As a vague scientific measure, I installed the upper partition so as to divide the house into two equal rectangles and I glued it in place. In time, I'll be able to see whether the birds exhibit any preference for one type of room or the other.

The Roof

Prior to the addition of the roof, some remaining timber work is added to the inside top edge of the dovecote. Two pieces of 480mm (18⅞in) and two pieces of 430mm (16¹⁵⁄₁₆in) batten are used to form a continuous inside edge. Use three 30mm (1¼in) screws per side to secure each piece.

The roof did not turn out to be the doddle I had envisaged and, although I am trying to give prescriptive instructions, it may take a little patience and sanding to end up with four triangular roof panels that actually fit together. I would strongly recommend the use of PU (polyurethane) wood adhesive and panel pins to help secure the roof along the seams whilst the glue is curing.

Start by cutting out the required panels from the 1400 × 500mm (55 × 19⅝in) piece of plywood. The two slightly smaller panels will inevitably have to fit inside the two larger panels. The panels are fixed so as to leave an overlap over the edge of the main body of the dovecote.

Start attaching the roof by fixing two similar panels in place on opposing sides. Use one central screw to hold each panel in place; position the screw about 30mm (1¼in) up from the bottom edge of each panel. Use a piece of tape across the top of both panels to hold the whole affair in position.

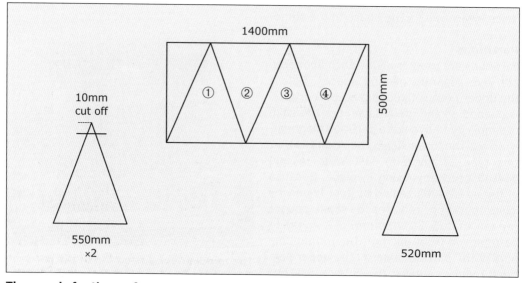

The panels for the roof are marked and cut as shown.

It is now a matter of offering the other panels into position and temporarily securing as previously described. You will have to adjust the positions of several of the boards until you find the magic point at which they all fit snugly together. When you reach the correct position, add another two screws to the bottom edge of each of the panels.

You can now manipulate the panels so as to add glue to the seams. I use PU glue in most of my constructions because it sets in about five minutes. It contains the same stuff as those cans of magic expanding foam that builders use to fill in gaps. If necessary, use panel pins to hold the edges of the roof sheets in position while the glue cures. When the glue is dry you will need to trim the excess away with a sharp knife and then give the joints a light sanding.

I finished off my roof by adding strips of flash band down the corners. As the roll of flash band is 100mm (4in) wide, I used a pair of scissors to cut a long strip in half down its length. The stuff is easy to cut; you can also fold it in half lengthways, thus leaving a crease line to act as a cutting guide.

The Supporting Bracket

You are left with two main options for putting your dovecote into service. You could drill two small holes near the top of the roof and hang the project from a suitable tree, bracket or beam. The best policy is to mount the house on top of a piece of 75 × 50mm (3 × 2in) or 100 × 50mm (4 × 2in) timber. Follow the recommendations in the cutting list or else cut your chosen piece of post timber to the length you desire. You will have to either concrete your post into the ground or nail it to an existing wooden gatepost or fence. The original prototype had included a much less robust bracket, which was found to be completely inadequate. This bracket is far more substantial and will hopefully stand up to strong wind.

Cut the two pieces of 280mm (11in) length so that ends of each respective piece are mitred inwards at 45 degrees, e.g. / \. Find the centre point of the previously drilled 450mm (17¾in) piece and nail it using 130mm (5in) nails across the top of the long post to form a T. The mitred lengths of timber can now be nailed in place as supports under each arm of the T. Position the mitred timbers and nail them to the main post first. You will now need to run the drill back through the existing holes on the top of the T so that the mitred supports are also drilled. Lastly, you can now add nails to the mitred bars where they join the underside of the T. Make sure that the nails do not interfere with the bolt holes. You can now bolt your post to the underside of the house using coach bolts, washers and nuts. On the random off-chance that your bolts are slightly too short, countersink the holes under the stand with a larger

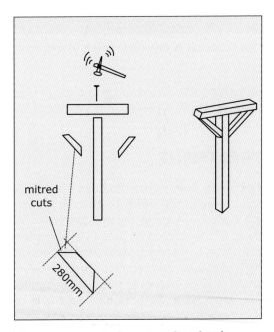

mitred cuts

280mm

The recommended support bracket is made from heavy timber as shown. Bolt the pole to a wall or gatepost.

The dovecote is finished. Perch blocks have been added underneath the lower doorways.

drill. Using this technique would mean that the nuts will be recessed into the timber by a small margin.

TREATMENT

I did use a sheet of plywood that had a reasonable grain and finish to it which left me the option of varnishing the dovecote. As most of the dovecotes that I've ever seen are white, I decided to stick with convention and eventually gave the project several coats of white non-drip gloss. If you're like me, you'll have plenty of half-used pots of paint kicking about from previous domestic painting jobs.

FURTHER SUGGESTIONS

I did think that a narrow piece of architrave or moulding painted black and running around the house at the middle level would have provided a visual enhancement to the design. I think I'd probably seen it somewhere else but as it served no practical purpose and my time was limited, I didn't get around to doing it. It's now the wrong time of year for me to offer my house to the local dove and pigeon population, so I won't be able to resolve the discussed partition issues. If it does become apparent that one section is favoured more than another, the roof can be removed and the design altered outside of the nesting season.

Chapter 6

Rabbit Hutch

RABBITS JUST AREN'T BRITISH!

The modern-day hobby of keeping rabbits as pets has largely evolved from what was once a very *en vogue* manner of producing meat for the kitchen table. Not only were the Normans largely responsible for bringing dovecotes into Britain, they also brought rabbits with them. How easy the modern-day farmer's life would be if it wasn't for hordes of rabbits and pigeons. Traditionally, farmed rabbit populations were kept in controlled areas; these were man-made warrens where they could live underground but be harvested at will. On many past travels around Dartmoor, I have encountered these man-made stone and earthen banked areas, still recognizable by both topography and name; Ditsworthy Warren is one that springs to mind. By the end of the eighteenth century, specific rabbit breeds were emerging and so with them, the divergence between what are regarded as showing or fancy rabbits and what are regarded as table breeds.

A rabbit is a relatively easy animal to keep and we all know that they will readily eat many of our vegetable offerings, some weeds and grass and a handful of commercial rabbit grub. The problems that many pet rabbits face must be those of loneliness and boredom. Like any animal, they will do better in pairs, even in some instances if the other animal isn't a rabbit – a guinea pig for instance! If you are thinking of getting a rabbit please bear in mind it doesn't want to spend all its life in the hutch, you'll have to let it out for a supervised run around the garden on a regular basis.

Guinea Pigs

As nobody ever goes shopping for a guinea pig hutch, this design will also be suitable for accommodating them. Guinea pigs are residents of the Andean areas of South America, where they are essentially the local equivalent of our wild rabbit. Their layers of thick fur and thick skin help to keep them warm on the extremely cold nights in the mountains. Unfortunately for them, they are on the menu of nearly every local restaurant and eatery in that part of the world. The South Americans even have government-sponsored breeding programmes to enhance the size of the various table breeds of Cuy (as they are known in Peru). I can attest that the flavour is nothing to shout about and the little blighter's are fiddly to eat. On the whole I think they are a lot better off as children's pets.

The Rabbit Hutch Design

As you next go past a pet shop, you'll inevitably see a plethora of small rabbit hutches for sale, usually piled up outside. We'll build our hutch a bit bigger than some of those little crates. We won't be going anywhere new with the design, we'll stick with the general lean-to configuration but we will have a separate darkened nesting area for the lucky incumbent.

CUTTING LIST AND MATERIAL REQUIREMENTS

Base

- One piece of 9mm ($\frac{3}{8}$in) ply cut to 1.2 × 0.6m (47$\frac{1}{4}$ × 23$\frac{5}{8}$in).

The following pieces of 50 × 25mm (2 × 1in) batten are required:

- Two pieces of 1.2m (47$\frac{1}{4}$in).
- Two pieces of 0.6mm (23$\frac{5}{8}$in).

Back

- One piece of 9mm ($\frac{3}{8}$in) ply cut to 1.22 × 0.45m (48 × 17$\frac{6}{8}$in).

Roof

- One piece of 9mm ($\frac{3}{8}$in) ply cut to 1.24 × 0.65m (49 × 25$\frac{1}{2}$in).

Sides

- Two pieces of 9mm ($\frac{3}{8}$in) ply cut to 550 × 600mm (47$\frac{1}{4}$ × 23$\frac{5}{8}$in).

The following pieces of 50 × 25mm (2 × 1in) batten are required:

- Two pieces of 410mm (16$\frac{1}{8}$in).
- Two pieces of 490mm (19$\frac{1}{4}$in).
- Two pieces of 500mm (19$\frac{5}{8}$in).

Partition

- One piece of 9mm ($\frac{3}{8}$in) ply cut to 510 × 600mm (47$\frac{1}{4}$ × 23$\frac{5}{8}$in).

The following pieces of 50 × 25mm (2 × 1in) batten are required:

- One piece of 230mm (9in).
- One piece of 350mm (13$\frac{3}{4}$in).
- One piece of 470mm (18$\frac{1}{2}$in).

- One piece of 495mm (19$\frac{1}{2}$in).

Front and Run Doors

- One piece of 9mm ($\frac{3}{8}$in) ply cut to 380 × 520mm (15 × 20$\frac{1}{2}$in).
- Two small squares of ply measuring 120 × 120mm (4$\frac{3}{4}$ × 4$\frac{3}{4}$in).

The following pieces of 50 × 25mm (2 × 1in) batten are required:

- One piece of 780mm (30$\frac{11}{16}$in).
- Two pieces of 420mm (16$\frac{1}{2}$in).
- Two pieces of 830mm (32$\frac{5}{8}$in).

Legs

- Four lengths of 50 × 25mm (2 × 1in) batten cut to 0.6mm (23$\frac{5}{8}$in).

Latches

- Two hook and eye sets are required.
- Turn-buckles are readily made out of small off-cuts of plywood.

Ancillary Items

Five hinges are needed. Three for the main run door and two for the nesting compartment door. Anything that you have in the way of hinges around the 40mm (1$\frac{1}{2}$in) mark will suffice.

HOW TO ASSEMBLE THE HOUSE

The Baseboard

Hopefully by now you've realized that each of the designs starts with a good sturdy reinforced baseboard and the rest of the design is built around that. With the components listed in the base cutting list, form a surround underneath the plywood floor. The four lengths of batten form a rectangle around the edge of the ply floor sheet. Drive fixings though the ply and into the

The hutch baseboard is made up as shown here.

timber underneath. The narrowest faces of the wooden battens are the ones in contact with the plywood in this instance. In many of the projects, where the individual components are made from plywood reinforced with wooden timber, I have opted to use nails to join the parts together. When it comes to assembling the different parts together, then use screws.

Preparing the Sides and the Partition

The two sides are made up in a similar manner. They will be positioned facing each other, one at either end of the hutch, both with their additional reinforcing batten facing inwards. The two side panels first need to be cut to give them a lean-to profile; the 600mm (23½in) edge is the bottom edge. The gradient is achieved by slicing off a 100mm (4in) deep wedge from the top edge of the panel. The front facing edge of the panel should measure 550mm (21⅝in) high but this will slope down to 450mm (17¾in) at the rear of the hutch. The illustrations should make this self-explanatory.

The lengths of batten now need to be added to the side panels. Orientate the panels so that the sloping edge is at the top. Use the 410mm (16⅛in) length of batten along the rear (450mm) edge. The 500mm (19⅝in) length goes along the front (550mm) edge and the piece of 490mm (19¼in) timber is used to brace the roof line. At the bottom of each panel there is a 40mm (1½in) gap between the bottom of the panel and the battening. If you are confused, remember that a picture paints a thousand words, read the instructions in conjunction with studying the photographs and diagrams.

The slightly smaller piece of plywood earmarked for the partition also needs its roof cut to match the slope of the two side panels. Again, this leaves us with a 100mm (4in) difference in height between the front and the rear edge. Use one of the side panels as a template, mark the described triangle for removal and cut it off with a saw. The other alteration to this panel is the removal of a section to provide a doorway to the nesting area. On my design I've removed a square section from the lower edge of the rear of the panel. The section for removal is square and measures 180 × 180mm (7 × 7in). I am aware that this door

The two sides and the partition are shown. The sides fit on the ends of the board. The partition is shorter because it sits on top of it.

will be too small for some of the larger types of rabbit – enlarge it if you wish.

The partition board now needs the addition of pieces of timber bracing. I have designed my hutch so that the nesting area is on the left of the house. The pieces of bracing batten should be added to the partition board so that when it is put in place, the batten is in the unseen nesting area, not in the visible run.

Arrange and fasten the following pieces of battening to the partition board as follows:

- The piece of 230mm (9in) fits on the vertical rear edge of the panel above the doorway.
- The piece of 350mm (13¾in) fits along the level of the floor.
- The piece of 470mm (18½in) fits against the front facing edge.
- The piece of 495mm (19½in) is the roof support.

Fitting the Sides and the Partition

Having made the side panels and partition, we can now start fitting them to the base. The sides will fit on to their respective baseboard positions and they can be screwed to the underlying timber work using four 30mm (1¼in) screws. The best way to describe the position of the partition is to use the piece of 780mm (30¹¹⁄₁₆in) batten (listed under cutting list – front) as a guide. This length of timber is used at the front of the hutch to reinforce the top edge and offer the roof some support. It fits between the tops of the partition and the right-hand side panel. On the right-hand side, it sits against the battening used to edge the panel, not against the plywood. Use this stick as a spacer to find and mark the correct position for the partition in relation to the right-hand side of the hutch.

After marking the position of the partition, fix the component in place by carefully drilling and driving screws through from

The sides and partition are fixed in place; the partition is screwed from underneath.

A top bar has been added at the front of the main compartment. This helps support the roof.

underneath the baseboard – easier said than done. The best method is to hold the partition in its correct place, draw around its footprint, remove the partition, drill three holes in the footprint that will allow screws to catch the timber reinforcing. Re-position the partition using your pencil marks and drive the screw in from underneath.

After you have fixed the partition in place, screw the described 780mm (30¹¹/₁₆in) batten in place between the partition and the right-hand side of the hutch. Position the bar so that it is flush forward but no part of it breaks the slope of the roof line. The screws go through the partition and the right-hand side and into the ends of the length of timber. You'll need to use 65–75mm (2½–3in) screws and will have to pilot drill the holes in order to get through the woodwork and into the ends of the length of batten.

The Back and Roof

The back panel can now be added, which will give the project its rigidity. Ensure that the top of the back panel is level with the top corners of each of the side panels. Screw the panel in place using fixings down each corner, ensuring that all is sitting squarely before you secure it. The panel can also be fastened to the back of the partition with two or three additional screws. The sheet is also fastened at regular intervals along the bottom edge where it overlaps the base unit.

It is now an appropriate point to add the roof. It should be evident that there is now plenty of timber on the top of the project to fasten it to. Position the roof sheet to give an equal overlap all the way around the hutch before adding screws. Put four 30mm (1½in) screws down through the roof into each of the ends and another four into the top of the partition. Add two or three additional screws along the front edge of the project. The back edge does

not have any additional timber but this can be resolved with a smear of PU wood glue prior to screwing the roof down.

The Project Grows Legs

Ensure that all the legs are the same size before you get started. I mitred all the ends of my legs purely for aesthetic reasons (looks). The legs are all mounted at the corners of the hutch and are positioned so that there is a clear 400mm (15¾in) of leg beneath the lowest part of the hutch. I used three 45mm (1¾in) screws per leg and just drove them straight through the multi layers of timber at the corners of the hutch.

Attach the legs in pairs, one end at a time and use a straight edge to ensure that the two leg ends are level. With a little careful

The legs are screwed into the corners of the house corresponding with the timber bracing inside.

measurement and care you should get it right first time so that the hutch doesn't wobble when you stand it up.

The Run Door

The main run door is almost a mini project in itself; that said, it's not difficult to make. The run door is made from four lengths of batten arranged in a rectangle. As the shape of the door depends on butt joints, you need to ensure that the four cut pieces of batten used to make this door have decent square cut ends. Arrange the four lengths of timber into a rectangle, the longer lengths fit inside the two shorter lengths. The corners are pilot drilled and screwed with 75mm (3in) screws.

Take the two small squares of plywood listed in the front section of the cutting list and cut them both diagonally across to leave four triangular sections of ply. These sections are used to make up the joints on the corners of the main hutch door. Use nails that are in the region of 1.5mm (approximately $\frac{1}{16}$in); these are about the next grade up from panel pins. Use nails that are at least 30mm (1$\frac{1}{4}$in) long; if they go right through the work don't worry, just turn the work over and bend the points back into the wood.

Having laid out your doorway in a rectangle, position a piece of plywood over a selected corner of the door. Try and envisage where the timber is underneath your plywood so that you get three nails into each piece of batten. Space each group of three nails in a triangle for added strength.

Additional strength is added to the door by covering it in wire. In this instance I elected to use galvanized weld mesh (square holes) because I had a suitable sized piece to hand. Chicken wire will suffice just as well. Measure your wire and cut it to fit, ensuring that any sharp points are either removed or folded over. The wire is fastened on to the door on what will be the

Butt joints are made by careful drilling of holes and long screws.

Corners can be reinforced by the addition of plywood bracing.

inward side. Use plenty of wire staples, space them at least one every 100mm (4in) to ensure that the incarcerated inhabitants don't get a start on unravelling the job.

The run door is secured at the right-hand side of the hutch and, because it is heavy, it needs three hinges. Attach the hinges to the door, set the outermost ones about 50mm (2in) in from the top and bottom. Hanging any door is an art form; hold the door against the run so that it sits nice and squarely. Work out where the top hinge rests against the hutch and try and mark

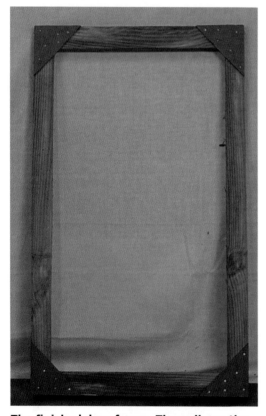

The finished door frame. The nails on the corner joints have been positioned so that there are six fixings driven through the ply into each corner. Each set of nails is in two groups of three so that each piece of underlying batten has three nails holding it.

the hutch accordingly. Using another loose hinge you should be able to work out the position of the screw holes in relation to the marks you have made.

To start with, hang the door with just one screw in the top hinge. You can now use this as a guide to alter the position of the other hinges so that the door closes properly. When you find the correct position for your door, add more screws as required.

The Sleeping Area Door

The door for the nest area is simply a piece of 380 × 520mm (15 × 20½in) plywood with hinges on the left hand edge. Use 12mm (½in) screws to secure the hinges to the plywood. It seemed like a worthy addition to add some ventilation holes to the upper portion of the door. I used a 25mm (1in) flat blade drill to drill a series of equidistant holes. You could use a smaller drill and drill a few more holes but ensure they are measured and evenly spaced if you want it to look reasonable.

When both doors are in the closed position, there is little or no space between them. Before screwing the nesting area door to the hutch, ensure that you have your hinges in a position that will allow both doors to fully close.

Turn-Buckles

The doors on the house are secured with simple turn-buckles made from small off-cuts of ply and timber. Two small ply pieces cut to 25 × 60mm (1 × 2½in) can be used to make a closure device for the nesting area and some heavier 25 × 25mm (1 × 1in) can be used to make a similar fastener for the main door. The pieces for the run door should be of increased length, 100mm (4in) is fine.

In addition to the turn-buckles, I've added an extra hook and eye to the top edge of each door. This will give a degree of added security to the doors.

Wooden turn-buckles secure the run and sleeping area doors.

The house is finished. A hook and eye secures the top of the run door. The other turnbuckles are sufficient to hold the front doors closed against rabbits.

FURTHER SUGGESTIONS

To date I haven't used the facility or indeed treated it, simply because I already have an obscene number of pigs, poultry and sheep, and I don't wish to become a keeper of rabbits as well. If I did wish for a rabbit to use my run, I would coat the hutch in Ronseal and cover the roof in a layer of heavy duty polythene, which could be stapled or glued on.

The doors close snugly against each other.

Chapter 7

Aviary

Aviaries are not cheap to either buy or manufacture, probably due to the large quantity of wire in them. This is rather a shame, as budgies have always been cheap enough. I have had budgies in the past and can thoroughly recommend them as being friendly, entertaining pets. The beauty of an aviary as a project, however, is that it is perhaps one of the easiest of the projects to make. Due to the modular nature of this design, it is not difficult to change the dimensions of the project allowing the builder to vary the end product to suit their own personal budget, budgie or space constraints. Bear in mind that if you intend to keep birds in an outdoor aviary, they need a lot more protection against the elements outside our summer months.

Standing with a tape measure in one hand, I set upon $1.5 \times 1.5 \times 0.75$m ($59 \times 59 \times 29\frac{1}{2}$in) as a design size that offered ample potential flying space with a footprint that wasn't so narrow that the whole thing would fall over.

As with the other projects, it's a case of getting plenty of 50×25mm (2×1in) roofing batten and a few off-cuts of plywood to make the corner reinforcements.

CUTTING LIST AND MATERIAL REQUIREMENTS

Front
- Two pieces of 50×25mm (2×1in) cut to 1.5m (59in).
- Four pieces of 50×25mm (2×1in) cut to 1.4m (55in).
- One piece of 50×25mm (2×1in) cut to 0.425m ($16\frac{3}{4}$in).

Back
An optional plywood back is described in the instructions.

- Two pieces of 50×25mm (2×1in) cut to 1.5m (59in).
- Four pieces of 50×25mm (2×1in) cut to 1.4m (55in).

Sides
- Four pieces of 50×25mm (2×1in) cut to 0.75m ($29\frac{1}{2}$in).
- Four pieces of 50×25mm (2×1in) cut to 1.4m (55in).
- Two pieces of 50×25mm (2×1in) cut to 0.65m ($25\frac{1}{2}$in).

Top
An optional plywood top is described in the instructions.

- Two pieces of 50×25mm (2×1in) cut to 1.6m (63in).

- Four pieces of 50 × 25mm (2 × 1in) cut to 0.65m (25½in).

Door
- Two pieces of 50 × 25mm (2 × 1in) cut to 0.7m (27½in).
- Two pieces of 50 × 25mm (2 × 1in) cut to 0.375m (14¾in).

Reinforcements
A number of plywood reinforcement pieces will be needed to help brace the joins and corners of the aviary. To make the triangular variety of brace, cut a 150 × 150mm (6 × 6in) square of 9mm (⅜in) plywood and then slice it diagonally in half to produce two triangular braces. To make the second type, of use on T butt joints, start with the same 150 × 150mm (6 × 6in) square of 9mm (⅜in) plywood then cut two of the corners off, as illustrated.

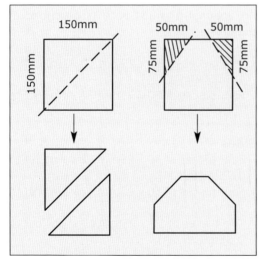

Bracing pieces for the corners of the aviary panels can be made up as illustrated.

Nesting Boxes
You may wish to add a couple of nesting boxes to your aviary; these can easily be manufactured from off-cuts of 9mm (⅜in) plywood.

- Two 120 × 150mm (4¾ × 6in) sides.
- Two 140 × 150mm (5½ × 6in) sides.
- One 140 × 140mm (5½ × 5½in) floor.
- One 145 × 160mm (5¾ × 6¼in) roof.

Perches
Perches can be made from cuttings or small branches from trees.

Ancillary Items
Screws of 7.6cm (3in) are required to secure the corners of each panel. A selection of fine nails 35–40mm (1¼–1½in) long are required to fasten the plywood bracing pieces to the framework. Three 40mm (1½in) hinges are needed for the run door. Two small sliding door bolts are required for door security. M6 coach bolts, nuts and washers are used to join all the separate panels of the aviary together. The run can be coated in fine chicken wire or weld-mesh; the latter is probably better suited but is significantly more expensive. Galvanized wire staples are needed to secure wire netting or mesh to the framework of the aviary.

PREPARATION

A level surface and either a set square or some other corner gauge are all that's required for success in this project. Some sort of gauge or template will ensure that you are fastening your panels together squarely. If you don't have a set square, mark and cut a piece of plywood to an accurate 90 degrees and use that as a template.

HOW TO ASSEMBLE THE HOUSE

Front

The two 1.5m (59in) pieces of 50 × 25mm (2 × 1in) make up the top and bottom rails of the panel: lie them flat on the floor, one above the other, and arrange the four 1.4m (55in) pieces of batten between them. Two of the bars are the side bars and

two are positioned at 0.5m (19⅝in) and 1m (39⅜in).

The remaining 0.425m (16¾in) piece of 50 × 25mm is the lintel of the doorway. Position this piece of batten 0.7m upwards of the 1.5m (59in) bottom bar. You can position the doorway between any of the three uprights to suit your requirements.

The four corners of the panel all need reinforcing using the triangular plywood corner pieces. The other four intersections should be reinforced using the other illustrated bracing piece. The two joints around the doorway lintel should also be reinforced using ply sections but on the opposite side (inside) of the panel.

After nailing on all the plywood reinforcing pieces, use an electric drill to pilot drill all the butt joints so that you can put two 75mm (3in) screws through each joint.

Prior to finishing the aviary panel, give it a lick of paint, if so desired. The final act is to add the all important bird-retaining wire

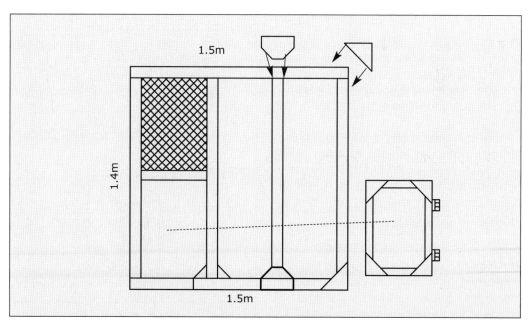

The front panel is the most complicated side but is not difficult to make. The bracing pieces around the doorway are on the inside.

to the run, after which painting or treatment becomes more difficult. Use sufficient staples to secure the wire at regular intervals.

Back

The back panel is constructed after the same fashion as the front panel. It is possible to do away with the need for a wire back panel and instead replace the wire covering with a layer of plywood measuring 1.5 × 1.5m (59 × 59in).

Sides

The two side panels are identical and each is made up from two uprights of 1.4m (55in), resting on and topped by two pieces of 0.75m (29½in) batten. The remaining two items from the cutting list are two lengths of 0.65m (25½in), which are infill pieces in the panel. Position these so that they are evenly spaced, 0.47m (18½in) from top and bottom of the panel.

Follow suit with reinforcing pieces and screwed butt joints before adding a covering of wire to the panels.

Top

The top can either be made from a single piece of plywood or the same technique as the other sections. If going with a plywood top, the size you will require is 1.6 × 0.75m (63 × 29½in).

From the cutting list, a wire top is constructed from two lengths of 1.6m (63in) with four pieces of 0.65m (25½in) set in between the two long battens; the short lengths make up the ends and two in-between bracing bars.

Door

The finished door is to fit inside the gap measuring 0.7 × 0.425m (27½ × 16¾in). The four pieces of batten should be arranged into a rectangle measuring 0.7 × 0.425m (27½ × 16¾in) so that when the door is complete, it will fit into the doorway.

Use ply reinforcing on the corners and wire the door accordingly. The door is hung on three hinges and bolts need to be added to the door top and bottom for maximum security.

Nesting Boxes

Nesting boxes are easy to make and require little more than some plywood off-cuts, panel pins and wood glue. The base is 140 × 140mm (5½ × 5½in) and the other sides can be tacked and glued on that.

Use a 120 × 150mm (4¾ × 6in) section for the back, which sits on the base. The other 120 × 150mm (4¾ × 6in) sections needs 25mm (1in) cutting off its length, thus reducing it to 125mm (4¹⁵⁄₁₆in), and a 40mm (1½in) hole drilling in it for the birds to get in. The two 140 × 150mm (5½ × 6in) sections of ply need both cutting to a 'lean-to' shape by removing a 25mm deep wedge off one of the shortest sides.

The roof 145 × 160mm (5¾ × 6¼in) can be secured in place with a single screw or

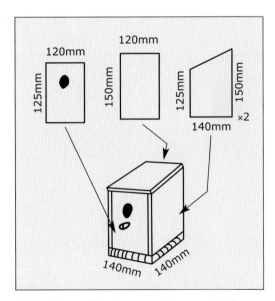

A simple nesting box can be up out of scraps of plywood left over from other projects.

The joints between the panels are made using coach bolts and are constructed as illustrated here.

The bolts need to be long enough to pass through 75mm of timber.

nail in the top edge; the roof may need removing for cleaning at some point. It's normal practice to add a small perch below the entrance hole of nesting boxes.

Fitting It Together

You may need two people for this job. The run panels are fastened together using M6 (6mm or ¼in) coach bolts, washers and nuts. You will need to work on a level surface. Bolts will need to be at least 80mm (3¼in) in length. Bolt the side panels to the large front and back panels using three bolts per corner. Pilot drill holes using a drill bit slightly larger than the bolt diameter prior to fixing the bolts in place. The front and back panels are 1.5m (59in) long and the end sections are bolted on to these panels, thus slightly increasing the overall length of the run. The roof should be secured using at least two bolts per side.

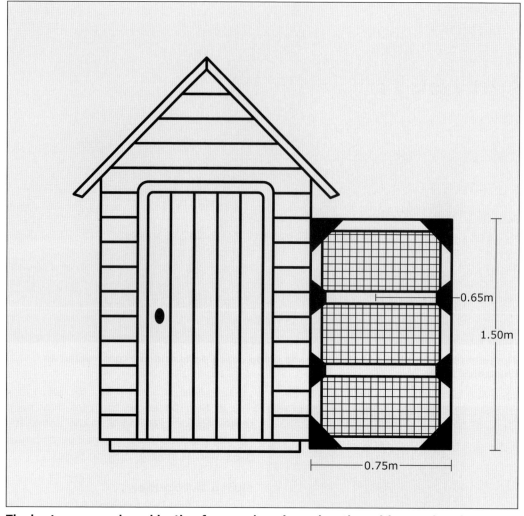

0.65m

1.50m

0.75m

The best year-round combination for an aviary, in conjunction with a garden shed.

FURTHER SUGGESTIONS

Aviaries are only any good in the warmer months of the year; it's just too cold and damp for most breeds of cage bird the rest of the year. Whilst we don't have the where-withal to show you how to build a complete shed, the best bird set-ups I have seen combine a small commercial shed that the birds can live in year round, with an outdoor aviary on the side of it.

Chapter 8

Ferret House

KEEPING FERRETS

Ferrets are essentially a working animal, although many people do just keep them as pets or for showing. It's widely thought that the animals were first introduced into this country by the Romans, who used them for hunting in much the same manner as today. The closest wild relation to the ferret is the polecat, although it's easy to see that they bear similarities to stoats, weasels and mink. The use of a working ferret has always been to aid control of wild rabbit populations, although they can also help in putting a meal on the table. Normal practice is to net the main entrances of a rabbit warren and then put the ferret in. The general idea is that the ferret will flush the rabbits out of the burrow, not catch them. When all goes to plan, the rabbits will attempt to escape and will be caught in the nets. The ferreter then has to do a humane job of killing the rabbits. When all goes to pot, the ferret may catch a rabbit underground, kill it, have a large dinner and then decide to have a lengthy sleep. Either the ferreter goes home without his animal or he gets his spade out and starts digging.

Having moved from a moorland area where the local rabbit population was completely out of control, letting ferreters on to one's land was to be on the receiving end of a very useful service. In hill country throughout the UK, the grass growing season is very much shorter than in lowland areas and it is widely reported throughout such districts that six rabbits can eat as much grass as one sheep. It should be clear therefore that rabbits are an economic nuisance to both the upland and lowland livestock farmer. It beggars belief that with such a large sustainable rabbit population throughout Great Britain, there is not more of it on the supermarket shelves.

The Ferret House Design

Ferrets are very energetic playful animals and they like to be kept amused. Bits of pipe and suchlike in the house will give them something to play with. This design is for a ferret house on two levels. There is a lower darkened nesting area and there are two ramps up to the top tier. There is a large weld-mesh covered door fronting the house. The two ramps give the animal the option of running a circuit around the house, as well as providing access between the levels. The house is on legs so that the nesting area is not sitting on a cold or damp floor.

CUTTING LIST AND MATERIAL REQUIREMENTS

Base and Floor

- Two pieces of 9mm (³⁄₈in) ply cut to 1.0 × 0.4m (39³⁄₈ × 15³⁄₄in).

The following pieces of 50 × 25mm (2 × 1in) batten are required:

- Four pieces cut to 350mm (13¾in).
- Four pieces of cut to 1.0m (39⅜in).

Sides

- The sides are cut from two pieces of 9mm (⅜in) ply measuring 0.8 × 0.42m (31½ × 16½in).

Roof and Back Panels

- The roof is cut from a piece of 9mm (⅜in) ply measuring 1.04 × 0.45m (41 × 17¾in).
- The back panel is cut from a piece of 9mm (⅜in) ply measuring 1.0 × 0.7m (39⅜ × 27½in).
- Two lengths of 50 × 25mm (2 × 1in) batten cut to 1.0m (39⅜in).

Matching Plywood

Before you start cutting the materials to make a project, ensure that where possible the grain of the plywood is matched in direction, at least on the visible faces of the project. It does look a bit odd if you have one side of a house with a horizontal grain and the other side with a vertical grain – not that the inmates worry too much. Also remember that many grades of ply are manufactured with one good face, the other often being distinctly mediocre.

Run Door

- Two pieces of 9mm (⅜in) ply cut to 120 × 120mm (4¾ × 4¾in).

The following pieces of 50 × 25mm (2 × 1in) batten are required:

- Two pieces cut to 265mm (10⅜in).
- Two pieces of cut to 1.0m (39⅜in).

Sleeping Area Door

- One piece of 9mm (⅜in) ply cut to 1.02 × 0.35m (40⅛ × 13¾in).

Ramps

- Two pieces of 9mm (⅜in) ply cut to 450 × 100mm (17¾ × 4in).

Legs

- Four pieces of 50 × 25mm (2 × 1in) batten cut to 750mm (29½in) are used to make the legs.

Latches

- Latches can be made from small 60 × 25mm (approximately 2½ × 1in) off-cuts of 9mm (⅜in) plywood.

Ancillary Items

Apart from the all important weld mesh required for the door panel (chicken wire is too flimsy for ferrets), a selection of 30 and 45mm (1¼ and 1¾in) screws is required. Four 40mm (1½in) hinges are needed for the doors and some 30–35mm (1¼–1½in) nails are needed to attach the plywood bracing to the corners of the main run door.

HOW TO ASSEMBLE THE HOUSE

The Baseboard

Start by assembling the two floorboards. The lower board is made up from one plywood panel with two pieces of 350mm (13¾in) and two pieces of 1m (39⅜in) batten arranged around the edges underneath. The four lengths of batten form a rectangle; nails are driven down through the board and into the batten underneath. Use a nail every 150mm (6in) or so.

The second floor board is made up in a similar fashion to the first one but the plywood is modified prior to adding the extra timbers. We are cutting two holes in the board, which will enable the ferrets to move between floors. Mark and remove two diagonally opposed corners as follows:

The lower floor is shown on the left; the upper floor with access holes is illustrated on the right.

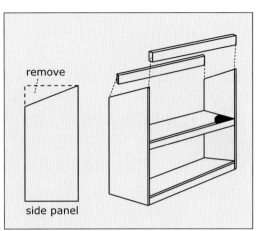

The floors are fixed between two side panels. Two top bars are added to support the roof.

- Measure and mark a 120 × 120mm (4¾ × 4¾in) square in the two chosen corners.
- Alter the geometry of each marked square by rounding off the corner nearest to the centre of the panel.
- Cut out the 'squares' using an electric jigsaw or other suitable manual saw.
- After adding the timbers underneath the base, you will need to reinforce the butt joints at the corners of the sections.
- Pilot drill two holes in each corner and use 45mm (1¾in) screws to tie the joints together.

Preparation and Fitting of the Sides and Baseboards

The side panels require some additional cutting to give them a 'lean-to' roof profile. The panels measure 0.8 × 0.42m (31½ × 16½in). Remove a 100mm (4in) wedge from the top edge of both panels so that instead of having two long sides measuring 0.8m (31½in), one side only measures 0.7m (27½in).

Working on a level surface, nail the two sides to the unmodified baseboard. The sides are fitted so that they completely cover the battening below the floor and are flush with the surface you are working on. Hopefully I'm stating the blindingly obvious that the front of the house is where the end panels are highest. The height at the back of the house is only 0.7m (27½in). Mark the midpoint (350mm or 13¾in) on the inward side of both of the side panels. These marks indicate the level of the upper floor. Align the surface of the plywood panel with these marks and fix the floor in place by nailing or screwing through the side panels. The nails or screws will drive into the battening underneath the ply floor. Use three or four fixings per side.

Ramps

The ramps are essentially made out of two off-cuts of plywood cut to 450 × 100mm (17¾ × 4in). The nimblest ferret will struggle to make ground up a bare plywood incline so you will either have to add rungs

Ramps are added to help the little critters get up and down.

or ridges or else cut grooves into your ramp. Ridges can be made from slithers of plywood glued on to the ramp at regular intervals. I opted to make controlled cuts in the ramps with an electric saw; this technique has created grooves that are 2–3mm (up to ⅛in) deep. These groves were made using a sliding cross-cut saw with a depth stop but this could equally be attained with a decent (tenon) hand saw. The grooves ended up spaced at little more than 25mm (1in) apart.

The ramps are fixed into position prior to adding further panels to the house. They are secured at the bottom edge with nails driven downwards through the floor. The top edges of the ramps are wedged into corners, so they shouldn't be able to move anywhere.

Fitting the Rear and Roof Panels

Prior to fitting further panels, there are two additional lengths of timber that need adding to the project. Select the two 1m (39³⁄₈in) lengths of 50 × 25mm (2 × 1in) batten and position them both as roof supports in between the two ends of the house. One length fits at the rear top edge of the house and the other at the front top edge. Both bars are positioned so that their narrowest 25mm (1in) faces are uppermost and both bars are in the highest possible position without breaking the line of the roof. The bars are mounted by drilling pilot holes through the side panels and into the ends of the bars. Both bars are mounted so as to be flush with the front and back of the house.

The rear panel can now be screwed into place, using 30mm (1¼in) fixings. There are three timbers to which the back panel is fixed. The first point of attachment is the top bar we have just described; the second line of attachment is the middle floor level; and the third line is the baseboard. Use a screw every 150mm (6in) along each line of fixings.

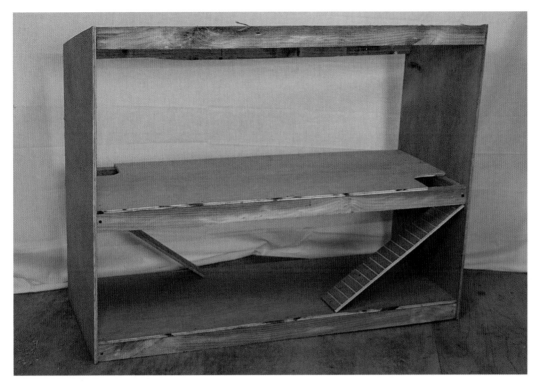

The ramps and top bars are in place. The house is ready for the rear and roof panels.

The roof should be positioned so that it is sitting squarely; screws are then added along the front and rear edges, they are driven down through the plywood into the batten rails beneath. A smear of glue can be added along the top edges of the ends prior to positioning and fixing the roof.

Legs

The legs are lengths of 50 × 25mm (2 × 1in) batten; all the legs are 750mm long and are mounted on the sides of the house. The legs protrude down 350mm (13¾in) beneath the house.

In keeping with the rabbit hutch project, the tops of the legs have been mitre cut at 45 degrees purely because I thought it looked better than a square-cut top. Use 45mm (1¾in) screws to secure the legs and position them so as to catch the substantial

timber work behind the plywood at mid and lower level. The top pair of screws are aligned and fixed into the middle floor timber. A second pair of screws is driven into the timbers beneath the lower floor. Each leg is fixed in the same manner. Use four screws per leg and drive them straight through the batten and into the layers of ply and timber at the corners of the hutch.

Work on one side at a time and use a straight edge to ensure that the (foot) ends of the legs are level. If when you stand the house up, one leg is not right, unscrew that leg and reposition it. Don't try to shorten legs by cutting them; Paddington Bear tried that in a story book I had years ago, after trimming all of the wobbly legs, I seem to recall he ended up with a footstool instead of a dinner table. Legs should definitely be repositioned rather than trimmed.

Legs have been added and the house really starts to take shape.

Run Door

The run door is made up from four pieces of batten arranged in a 1 × 0.365m (39³⁄₈ × 14³⁄₈in) rectangle. The two pieces of 120 × 120mm (4³⁄₄ × 4³⁄₄in) ply are cut diagonally into triangles and used to reinforce the corners of the run door. Ensure that the four pieces of batten have square-cut ends. Use 30mm (1¼in) nails that are in the region of 1.5mm (approximately ¹⁄₁₆in) thick, these are a little more substantial than panel pins. Position a piece of bracing ply over a corner of the door. Try and get three nails into each piece of batten. Repeat the exercise on all the other corners.

Cover the inside of the door in weld mesh. Chicken wire will not suffice for ferrets; it may last a while but a particularly rowdy animal will soon get to unravelling it. Whilst ferrets can't generally chew through wire, they will continually rive at it thus exposing any weaknesses. Measure your wire to fit and trim off any sharp points. Use galvanized wire staples to secure the mesh and space them at a rate of one every 100mm (4in) to ensure strength.

By way of a change, the door is secured to the house using two hinges along its top edge; set the hinges 100mm (4in) inward of each end. The hinges are fastened to the length of batten running across the top of the house.

The Sleeping Area Door

The door for lower floor nest area has been modified by the addition of a series of four ventilation holes along the top of the sheet. I used a 25mm (1in) flat-bladed drill to make my perforations. You could use a drill that's smaller and make more holes but please do ensure that the spacing of said holes is measured and not just random.

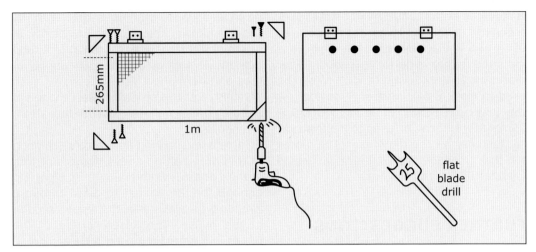

The two doors are hinged at their top edges and are made up as illustrated.

The door is again hinged along its top edge using a couple of 40mm (1½in) hinges. Use 12mm (½in) screws to secure the hinges to the plywood and 30mm (1¼in) screws to attach the hinges to the woodwork.

Turn-Buckles

Both doors on the house are secured using turn-buckles made from off-cuts of ply and timber used in the project. There is a single device securing the upper door, this

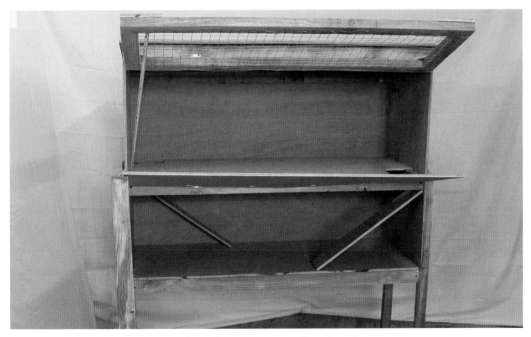

The house is all but finished; there is easy access for cleaning.

is mounted at the centre point on the lower (opening) edge. The lower door is secured using two similar devices, each of which is mounted either side of the door. Four pieces cut to 25 × 60mm (1 × 2½in) can be used to make a pair of closure devices for the lower area and some heavier 25 × 25mm (1 × 1in) can be used to make a similar fastener for the main door. The pieces for the run door should be of increased length, 100mm (4in) is fine.

FURTHER SUGGESTIONS

The roof could be covered if necessary and the project can be treated or painted as desired. Please remember that with all caged animals, they do require plenty of attention if they are to remain fit and healthy. As well as an adequate supply of feed and permanent access to water, such animals require a constant clean change of bedding and regular removal of litter from the house.

Ferrets love larking about, so a selection of toys wouldn't go amiss. A piece of tree branch and a suitable length of pipe, big enough for the animal to crawl through, wouldn't be wasted in the upper section of the house. The lower portion of the house will be mainly used for sleeping so should be supplied with straw or shredded newspaper.

The doors in the closed position showing the fasteners that secure them.

Chapter 9

Quail Housing

And now for something completely different.... Many of you may never have set eyes on a quail, let alone considered keeping them. In terms of shape, I suppose the type of bird they most closely resemble are the game birds: grouse and partridge. Whilst quail may bear certain resemblances to other larger game birds, they themselves are in fact much smaller. A quail is certainly best described as a bird in the hand – a fairly small one at that.

WHY KEEP QUAIL?

Perhaps the most remarkable thing about the quail is its incredibly rapid life cycle. Let me give you some idea. You go out and buy yourself a quad of breeding birds, bring them home and put them in your newly built quail house. Most days you are getting three eggs a day. On about day eighteen, you decide to put all your eggs (we'll say

---

Quails Eggs

Considered to be a great delicacy, quails eggs are marginally bigger than a decent-sized acorn. Whilst that may not seem a lot, it's a fair-sized egg for a little bird and it goes very nicely in a sandwich. Quails eggs are seen pickled, bottled and sometimes fresh. They are a worthy addition to mixed salads where they can be added boiled and peeled. (Culinary tips in a DIY book, whatever next!)

---

fifty for arguments sake) in one basket. That basket is put into an incubator where in seventeen or eighteen days time, the eggs start to hatch. An 80–90 per cent hatch rate is not uncommon. When a quail hatches from its egg, it's about as big as a large bumble bee; within a few days, it is able to fly. Providing the newly hatched chicks are cared for correctly, at about six weeks old they will start to lay. Little more than eleven weeks has passed since you first bought your quail, and now you are now getting over forty eggs a day.

Whilst I'm not advocating that you all go and try the above experiment, I will freely admit that I did and learned a hell of a lot about the birds in the process.

There are several varieties of quail; the type I'm used to are *Coturnix japonica* or Japanese Quail. They are hardy little birds who thrive on a little chick crumb and clean water and lay prodigious quantities of eggs. You can expect in excess of 300 eggs a year from decent egg-laying strains. This quantity of eggs out of such a small bird does take its toll; whilst you may see life expectancies of quail banded around as up to three years, the reality is that many birds do not last two. The reason for this is they practically lay themselves to death. The quail is not a timid bird, neither is it flighty, preferring to spend much of its existence on the ground. Before we had children, we used to occasionally let them out in the house. They didn't appear to get overly upset at being manhandled and they weren't too difficult to catch when it came to putting them back in their house. What I will say is that the biggest problem that we have faced whilst keeping quail is singly and most certainly rats. For some reason, rats don't seem to be able to leave quail alone. If they find yours, they will destroy the lot, eating holes in your house, if necessary, in the process of gaining entry. I have found birds in a terrible state of repair after attacks by rats, but you may be surprised to learn that the only thing on par to being as damaging to the birds as vermin, is the male quail itself.

We did get to a point where we had only one female left and we made the mistake of keeping her in with the male too long. If birds are kept in fours or fives, then the male seems to have plenty of choice over which to divert his attentions without singling out one individual. If you leave a male in with one or two ladies, you'll certainly find that he will mercilessly tread, peck and generally harass them, even to the extent that one of our birds once lost an eye. It's a relatively common occurrence to find one of your laying birds with a bald or even bleeding head, where she's had all her head feathers pulled out in a fit of testosterone-fuelled malevolence. The males really are feisty little fellows.

So why keep quail? I would say that they are great entertainment with charming little characters and they do lay very tasty eggs. Whilst the quail egg is only small, it is very beautiful with its mottled colourful shell and they are considered a great delicacy. Quails themselves are regarded as something of a fanciful meal in themselves but as I eat a large portion, I can't say that I'd consider sacrificing three or four of my little birds just on the table of gluttony; the eggs seem a far better bet to me. In fact, I'll cut to the woodwork by saying that quails' eggs are in demand in most areas,

if you can find the right catering contacts. This could be a business opportunity waiting to happen. Then again...

The Quail House Design

You can keep quail in an aviary but sooner or later, a rat will get in. As they don't do a lot of flying, it is a relatively common practice to find them in rabbit hutches and suchlike. Over the years, I've trialled a number of quail house designs and this one I'd describe as being adequate for the job. The house has a small door, so that you can get the food and water in and out without the birds escaping. The house design also has a wooden pull-out droppings tray that is a great boon to the necessary regular cleaning routine required when keeping quail. If you are wondering where the nest box is, there isn't one. In our experience, quail will lay their eggs anywhere, hence the need to keep the floor free from a build-up of droppings.

CUTTING LIST AND MATERIAL REQUIREMENTS

Top and Bottom
- Two pieces of 9mm ($\frac{3}{8}$in) ply cut to 1 × 0.4m ($39\frac{3}{8}$ × $15\frac{3}{4}$in).

Back
- One piece of 9mm ($\frac{3}{8}$in) ply cut to 1 × 0.42m ($39\frac{3}{8}$ × $16\frac{1}{2}$in).
- One 0.4m ($15\frac{3}{4}$) piece of 50 × 25mm (2 × 1in) batten.

Sides
- Two pieces of 9mm ($\frac{3}{8}$in) ply cut to 0.4 × 0.4m ($15\frac{3}{4}$ × $15\frac{3}{4}$in).

The following pieces of 50 × 25mm (2 × 1in) batten are required:

- Four pieces cut to 400mm ($15\frac{3}{4}$in).

- Four pieces cut to 300mm (11$^{13}/_{16}$in).

Tray
- One piece of 9mm ($^{3}/_{8}$in) ply cut to 0.93 × 0.37m (36$^{5}/_{8}$ × 14$^{1}/_{2}$in).
- A thin strip of wood measuring 930 × 15 × 10mm (36$^{5}/_{8}$ × $^{6}/_{8}$ × $^{3}/_{8}$in).

Front
The following pieces of 50 × 25mm (2 × 1in) batten are required:

- One piece of 935mm (36$^{13}/_{16}$in).
- Two pieces of 335mm (13$^{3}/_{16}$in).

Door
- One piece of 9mm ($^{3}/_{8}$in) ply cut to 345 × 185mm (13$^{1}/_{2}$ × 7$^{1}/_{4}$in).

Latch
- A latch is made from two small plywood off-cuts measuring 25 × 60 and 25 × 80mm (1 × 2$^{3}/_{8}$ and 1 × 3$^{1}/_{8}$in).

Ancillary Items
Apart from plenty of 30mm (1$^{1}/_{4}$in) screws and some similar sized fine nails, the other notable hardware required is a couple of pieces of weld mesh or chicken wire to fit over the front. I've elected to use weld mesh as the finish looks marginally neater and this house may spend part of its life indoors. Four 75mm (3in) screws are used in the construction of the front section and four 12mm ($^{1}/_{2}$in) screws are needed to secure a pair of 40mm (1$^{1}/_{2}$in) hinges to the door.

HOW TO ASSEMBLE THE HOUSE

Preparation of the Side Panels
Start the project by making up two identical side panels. Arrange two lengths of 400mm (15$^{3}/_{4}$in) and two of 300mm (11$^{13}/_{16}$in) into a

Two side panels are made up as shown.

square. The shorter pieces fit inside of the longer pieces. Place a piece of 0.4 × 0.4m (15$^{3}/_{4}$ × 15$^{3}/_{4}$in) ply on top of the square and nail the lot together. Make sure you get three nails through the ply into each piece of batten.

Attaching the Top, Bottom and Back
The two side panels can now be screwed to the top and bottom sheets. The side panels sit in between the top and bottom sheets of plywood. Position one of the side panels at right angles to a sheet of 1 × 0.4m (39$^{3}/_{8}$ × 15$^{3}/_{4}$in) ply and after ensuring all the edges are flush, drive screws through the plywood and into the battening. Repeat this step for the other end of the sheet. We'll call this the baseboard.

There is the addition of a single piece of 0.4m (15$^{3}/_{4}$in) piece of 50 × 25mm (2 × 1in) batten, which acts as a bracing bar for the back panel. This piece is positioned halfway along the rear edge of the baseboard and

The panels are secured to a sheet of ply and an extra length of timber is added to help brace the back panel.

is fixed in an upright position. Use a fine drill bit to pilot drill two holes in the plywood, space the holes about 12mm (½in) apart. These holes go through the ply and into the end of this piece of batten.

Add the remaining top panel in a similar fashion to the first one. Use plenty of screws along the end joins and pilot drill two holes (as just described) to catch the end of the halfway bracing bar.

It is now a simple job to position and fix the back panel in place. Use screws to fix the panel into position; secure the back panel at both ends of the house and also along the halfway point, where the screws will catch the bracing bar.

The Door

We used to keep some quail in a house similar to this design. That particular quail house sat upon a small table outside the back door of our hovel in the hills. There was a day when my wife came in mortified to say that, as she had put the food into the

Careful pilot hole drilling and 75mm (3in) long screws are required to make up the front section.

cage, a quail had slipped past her and had flown off. Believe it or not, they fly like a rocket; straight up and away. The best principle is to keep the doorway of your cage fairly small thus cutting down the chances of inadvertent escapees. Alternatively, don't keep them outside.

The doorway is made from three pieces of timber that, when in position, allow for a slot underneath in which the droppings tray can be fitted. Select the 935mm (36¹³⁄₁₆in) long piece of timber; measure and mark the halfway point. This piece will be mounted across the face of the house allowing for a 15mm (⅝in) gap beneath it. The two pieces of 335mm (13³⁄₁₆in) batten are fastened as uprights in-between this rail and the roof. The spacing of the two shorter lengths of timber forms the doorway to the house. The gap between these two uprights is set at 120mm (4¾in). It's a matter of personal preference whether or not you require the front of your house to be symmetrical with the doorway directly in the middle. In a fit of indifference, I offset my doorway to the left-hand side. I used the centre point as a guide for positioning my right-hand doorpost.

The two short lengths of timber are attached to the longer 935mm (36¹³⁄₁₆in) piece prior to the component being fitted to the house. Both the joints require pilot drilling and two 75mm (3in) screws. The item is arranged and made up so that all the widest (50mm/2in) faces of the batten are facing the builder. It should be evident that 75mm (3in) screws are necessary to make the joints because they have to pass through the 50mm (2in) face of the longer batten before they can make contact with the two shorter timbers.

When the doorway structure is ready, it can be positioned in the front of the house so that it is flush with the forward edges of the plywood house. If the component has been made and aligned correctly, there should be a gap running all the way across the house underneath the lower piece of batten. The doorway component is fastened in place by driving screws through the plywood house into the ends of the batten. There are four points of attachment and you should pilot drill and get two screws into every joint.

The front is now in place. Note the slot at floor level; this is wide enough to allow a tray to be inserted into the house.

Door and Latches

The door is nothing more elaborate than a rectangular piece of plywood. Use the 12mm (½in) screws to secure the hinges to one side of the door. It is marginally easier to add the wire front to the house prior to fixing the door in position. Cut two sections of wire or mesh to fit your house. The sections are fixed in place using galvanized wire staples.

Staple Gun

I did experiment with using conventional fine wire staples to secure chicken wire to wooden batten and plywood. I used a staple gun with approximately 12mm (½in) wide staples. The hit/miss rate was about 50/50. Some staples penetrate the wood, some just buckle. On a project that might be kept indoors such as this, it's a quick method of getting the front on. For outside projects, don't bother, the staples will soon rust away.

The position of the door needs to take into account the space that is required for a small latch to be added to one side of it. I made up my latches using small off-cuts of plywood. Make up the latch first and then add the door afterwards is the best advice.

Tray

A suitable piece of ply is used to make up a removable tray that will enable a large proportion of the bird muck to be removed without opening the house. Push your tray into the opening and you will notice that: (a) it won't go right to the back because of the piece of timer bracing the back; (b) the slot into which the tray slides is 6mm (¼in) bigger than the tray. The former point can be resolved by marking the position of the 50 × 25mm (2 × 1in) bracing bar against the inserted tray; then remove a piece to suit thus allowing the tray to be pushed further back. The second point is necessary to

The wire has been added, the door is mounted and a latch has been put in place to hold the door closed.

The full extent of the tray can be seen. Note the notch out of the rear edge that allows the tray to fit over the back-panel support.

allow the removal of droppings but it also had a downfall in that it allows muck and detritus to be kicked out by the birds. To remedy this, a strip of wood is carefully doctored to plug the slot that the tray slides into. This strip of wood is then carefully screwed to the leading edge of the plywood tray. In the closed position, the tray will now extend all the way to the back of the house and the gap at the front of the house will be sealed off by the added strip of timber.

I cheated, I found a piece of quarter-profile beading that fitted the slot perfectly and so I used that instead of cutting a fresh piece. I also added two screws to the leading edge of the tray; these were set about 400mm (16in) apart so that I could use them as small handles to slide the tray in and out. Not pretty but pretty functional.

The tray is in place, the front edge is thick enough to completely plug the slot when the panel is fully inserted.

Finished and ready to go. By giving the tray a thicker front edge, the amount of debris kicked out on to the floor by the birds will be minimized.

FURTHER SUGGESTIONS

The project is essentially an indoors and fair weather item and so any painting or treatment is purely for cosmetic purposes. The project might lend itself to having some legs added to the design. I suppose that the house would also make a reasonable bird house that could be used in conjunction with the aviary project for budgerigars and suchlike.

You can buy small plastic pots with hooks on the back that will suffice for water and food. The trouble with quail is that they love to scratch in the same manner as chickens. You will find that soon after you have filled their feed container up, they will jump into it and kick the stuff everywhere. That usually means all over the floor outside the cage as well. It helps if you don't fill the food trays to the top.

Quail need a high-protein diet if they are to carry on laying eggs. The best commercially available feed is chick crumb, which is used for rearing chickens. What you may find is that your nearest supplier only stocks chick crumb between the spring and the autumn; I've run into this problem before. You can feed your quail layers pellets for a time but you'll have to give each portion a short blast in the food processor before you feed it to them. This is simply to break the pellets up into smaller grains that the birds can handle.

Quail love to wallow around in a bit of sawdust. Get some from a local joiner's workshop or sawmill. Every couple of days pull out the built-in tray and scrape it off to get rid of the build-up of droppings . Throw in a handful of sawdust and watch the birds come to life. On a previous project, I did create a nesting area for the quail to lay their eggs in but it proved to be a waste of time. Quail seem to lay their eggs anywhere, which is why you must avidly try to keep the house clean.

Chapter 10

Duck House

DUCKS

It was the infamous Basil Fawlty who said 'If you don't like duck then you're a bit stuck'. Of course he was referring to the cooked variety. Owing to a slightly curved bill, ducks always seem to me to look happy – I certainly wouldn't say the same of my geese. Both ducks and geese are an interesting addition to any smallholding or large garden, and it should come as little surprise that they are available in more strains, colours, shapes and sizes than you could possibly imagine. Where chickens will rip a garden to pieces, ducks have more interest in rooting out slugs, snails and other insects than tearing the borders to pieces. There are four principal reasons why one might wish to start keeping ducks: eggs, meat, ornamental/pet or decoy.

Eggs

It's a fact that some strains of duck (most notably Khaki Campbell and Indian Runner ducks) will lay 300 eggs a year; that's way in excess of the average chicken. As with many types of chicken, the problem with selecting ducks for egg-laying is that even within a breed, no two strains are the same. Some Khaki Campbells will lay furiously, whilst another strain will not. In order to find yourself decent egg-layers, you will first have to find someone else who has a strain that lay well and either buy stock from them or some fertile eggs for hatching. For those who aren't sure, Khaki Campbells are a khaki-coloured medium-sized bird, renowned for their egg-laying ability. They were originally bred from Mallard and Indian Runner ducks, with a bit of French Rouen duck thrown in for good measure. The Indian Runner duck is an extremely odd sight to the uninitiated or to the first-time cursory glance. The duck has a long neck, stands incredibly upright (a bit like a penguin) and obviously, as befitted by the name, they run everywhere. Indian Runners are available in a variety of colours and are also very good layers.

Meat

I love a bit of cooked duck with a slice of orange but owing to the previously discussed general theory on how happy a duck looks, it does make me feel particularly murderous when slaughtering them. I don't feel the same way about chickens or geese. If you want to keep ducks for meat, you will have to find somewhere that sells them at a day old or else start your own breeding programme. I haven't kept ducks exclusively for meat but I do know plenty of people that do; the most favoured breeds in my area are Aylesbury and Muscovy ducks. Aylesbury ducks are the large white old English breed found floating on many a village pond, they are relatively slow growing, although ducks hatched in the spring can easily be reared in time for Christmas.

Muscovy ducks are a different species altogether; for starters, they are adept fliers and like to perch on things. A former next-door neighbour had a duck tree, all his Muscovy would all perch in it at bed time – the upside was that the fox didn't get any. They grow to a substantial size, although I have been told that the meat can taste a bit gamey; that said, it is probably just how you feed them. In my opinion Muscovy ducks are ugly brutes with large patches of red skin around their faces; I suppose what they lack in aesthetics, they make up for in productivity. The next-door neighbour never bothered to incubate any and he always had plenty to sell at Christmas.

Ornamental, Call and Decoy Ducks
Many years ago, the rich and landed started breeding strains of domesticated ducks in order to entice wild ducks on to their properties for the purposes of shooting. The ducks would live on a pond or lake with shooting hides close by. As the wild birds would fly in they'd meet a sticky end: bang bang bang. Decoy ducks are now popularly known as call ducks and are available in a variety of shapes, colours and sizes. More often than not, they are bred to the duck equivalent of bantam size (there may be exceptions). Call ducks are mainly kept for ornamental purposes; good birds are costly; at poultry auctions I've seen them change hands for hundreds of pounds, even an average pair will be fifty to sixty pounds.

Keeping the Birds Happy
Ducks like to waddle around the garden so that they can root out insects and grubs. Anyone who has visited a pond or river with a bag of bread will have witnessed them dabbling around, tails in the air, searching for underwater edibles. There appears to be plenty of green stuff in their diet, although as previously cited, they lack the destructive power of chickens. You can buy formulated foods for ducks, which may be of value if egg quantity is what you are after. Most people feed their ducks on wheat or bags of mixed flaked maize and grain. When you feed your birds is up to you. I used to feed mine twice a day but of late I've cut all my feeds to once a day (in the morning). If you are fattening ducks for meat, then obviously you will have to follow a different regime.

Ducks like a secure little hut with a nice ramp that they can waddle up; the ramp doesn't want to be too steep. As they soil wherever they are standing and quickly paddle it all in, you need to keep on top of the cleanliness of the hut. Regular inputs of straw and regular cleaning-out is the answer. Somewhere amongst this melée, the ducks will lay their eggs. Eggs don't respond well to being caked in ducky muck – bacteria can get inside the egg; to prevent this you will need to collect your eggs regularly. Accessibility to the inside of the shed is paramount in order to aid speedy cleaning and help egg removal.

Water Management
The big snag with ducks is this – they need to have a pond. If you have a little pond, they will quickly turn it into a green soup and they will kill all signs of life that are in it. If you have a source of running water, or a pond with water flowing through it, keeping ducks is not a problem. Likewise, if you have a large pond or lake, the established ecosystem is well able to cope with the added nutrients from the duck muck. You can keep ducks in a small pond but they will need the water changing on a regular basis. If you have a large pond, one added benefit is that the birds will use the water for protection from foxes and other such vermin. Duck islands, either natural or artificial (as made famous by the MP expenses debacle in 2009) do actually serve a practical purpose

in protecting birds from predators; just don't put one on the company accounts.

Wing Clipping

If you hatch and rear a duck on your premises, they will know that your abode is also theirs. Occasionally they might go for a fly but they will usually come back. We had a duckling given to us that grew into a strapping young drake. He would often take off for a few forty-miles-an-hour circuits of the house, our hearts would flutter during the shooting season. Whilst being an impeccable aviator, unfortunately his credentials did not extend to road awareness – he got run over and, not wanting to waste a lightly damaged carcase, I forsook my principles and ate him. If you don't want your birds to fly, then you must clip their wings.

CUTTING LIST AND MATERIAL REQUIREMENTS

Base

- One piece of 9mm (³⁄₈in) ply cut to 1.0 × 0.5m (39³⁄₈ × 19¹¹⁄₁₆in).
- Three pieces of 75 × 50mm (3 × 2in) cut to 0.5m (19¹¹⁄₁₆in).

Sides

- To be cut from two pieces of 9mm (³⁄₈in) ply cut to 0.5 × 0.6m (19¹¹⁄₁₆ × 23⁵⁄₈in).

The following pieces of 50 × 25mm (2 × 1in) batten are required:

- Two pieces cut to 0.4m (15³⁄₄in).
- Two pieces cut to 0.45m (17³⁄₄in).
- Two pieces cut to 0.55m (21⁵⁄₈in).

Roof and Back Panels

- One piece of 9mm (³⁄₈in) ply cut to 1.02 × 0.5m (40¹⁄₈ × 19¹¹⁄₁₆in) – back panel.
- One piece of 9mm (³⁄₈in) ply cut to 1.04 × 0.55m (41 × 21⁵⁄₈in) – roof panel.

Frontal Timbers, Door and Ramp

- One piece of 9mm (³⁄₈in) ply cut to 0.75 × 0.6m (29¹⁄₂ × 23⁵⁄₈in) – door.
- One piece of 9mm (³⁄₈in) ply cut to 0.45 × 0.26m (17³⁄₄ × 10¹⁄₄in) – ramp.
- One piece of 9mm (³⁄₈in) ply cut to 0.12 × 0.26m (4³⁄₄ × 10¹⁄₄in) – vent panel.

The following pieces of 50 × 25mm (2 × 1in) batten are required:

- One piece cut to 1m (39³⁄₈in).
- One piece cut to 0.51m (20¹⁄₁₆in).

Latches

The house is kept secure using three turn-buckle latches made from off-cuts of plywood. Alternatively, brass turn-buckles or steel hook and eye sets could be used. All methods are inexpensive.

Ancillary Items

Aside from a suitable selections of nails and screws, the only other hardware used in this project is five 40mm (1¹⁄₂in) hinges. A selection of 12mm (¹⁄₂in) screws will be required to secure the hinges to the plywood.

HOW TO ASSEMBLE THE HOUSE

The Baseboard

Use the three lengths of 75 × 50mm (3 × 2in) timber to support the plywood base sheet. One length of timber is fastened underneath each end and one length in fixed under the middle. The timbers are fixed with their narrowest (50mm or 2in) face in contact with the plywood. Drive three screws down through the ply into each of the timbers.

Preparation and Fixing of the Side Panels

The two pieces of ply used for the end panels need modifying to a lean-to roof profile.

The overall height of the panel is 0.6m (23⅝in). A 100mm (4in) wedge needs removing from one end of the panel so that the finished article will measure 0.6m (23⅝in) at the front, reducing to 0.5m (19¹¹⁄₁₆in) at the rear.

The edges of the two panels can now be reinforced with pieces of 50 × 25mm (2 × 1in). Don't forget that the panels are manufactured so that when the sections are placed side by side, the reinforcing timbers are on the inward facing side of both panels.

Familiarize yourself with one of the plywood side sheets: the sloping side is the top

and the longest side is the front of the panel. The reinforcing pieces are arranged so that they are flush with the top, rear and front edges of the sheet. This means that the timbers do not extend all the way to the bottom of the sheet. You should ensure that the gap between the battening and the bottom edge of the sheet measures the same for both the front and back edges. This gap will be approximately 40mm (1½in).

Use nails or 30mm (1¼in) screws to fasten the battening to the plywood. The ends

Getting Your Ducks Home
For those who are not aware, ducks are awesome fliers. When you get any new birds home you either need to clip their wings or keep them in an enclosed run until they work out where food and bed is. Simply launching a duck on to your pond because there are some others on it won't work. Nine times out of ten, the ducks will simply clear off. It's a costly mistake that I've made once.

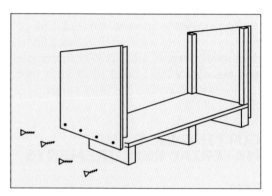

The panels are held in place with screws into the base supports.

Side panels and the base for a duck house.

can now be fitted to the baseboard using screws. Sit the side panels on to the base; the bottom edge of the panels should overlap the ends of the baseboard. Drive screws through the panels and into the supports that are under the baseboard.

Attaching the Rear

The rear panel is fixed to the back using 30mm (1¼in) screws. Use four screws per end. Ensure that the project is square and true prior to fixing the second edge in place. Additional fixings can be added along the bottom edge; one at each end and one in to the middle floor support.

Attaching the Roof

It is necessary to add two additional pieces of woodwork prior to fixing the roof in place. Add the 1m (39⅜in) length of 50 × 25mm (2 × 1in) batten as a top bar; this piece fits between the end panels at the front of the project. Position the bar so that the widest face is outward and the bar is up as high as it can go without breaking the line of the roof. Fix the bar in position with a couple of screws in each end; pilot drilling the holes is advisable to prevent splitting the wood.

The 0.51m (20¹⁄₁₆in) length of batten fits in an upright position between the top bar and the floor. This vertical bar is positioned so as to leave a 200mm (8in) gap (doorway) to the left of it. The measurement relates to a gap of 200mm (8in) from post to post. The upright is fixed in place with two 75mm (3in) long screws from the top and two 40mm (1½in) screws from underneath. Pilot drill the holes prior to fixing. The roof can now be fixed in place. Use screws to fasten both ends of the roof to the respective heavy woodwork on the side panels. Use three screws per side panel. It will also be possible to fasten the front edge of the roof to the wooden rail that was previously positioned along the top of the project. Use four or five evenly spaced fixings, as required.

A top bar to support the roof and a doorpost have been added.

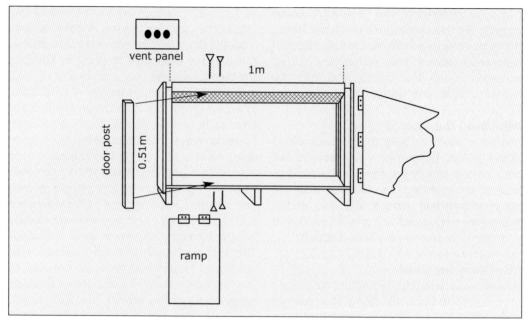

A vent panel, a ramp and one large door complete the front of the project.

House Doors

The house has a ramp and a larger door to aid cleaning. The large door is hinged on the right-hand edge with three 40mm (1½in) hinges. Set the hinges 50mm (2in) inward of the top and bottom edges of the

The middle of the three fasteners rotates and so can secure both ramp and door.

door, the remaining one should go in the middle. Use 12mm (½in) screws to fix the hinges to the plywood. Use 30mm (1¼in) screws to fix the door and hinges to the door post.

The smaller piece of plywood, 0.12 × 0.26m (4¾ × 10¼in), is used to make a vent panel. I used a 25mm (1in) flat-bladed drill to make three equally spaced holes in the panel. If you don't have a drill this big, mark out a regular pattern of smaller holes and drill them. The vent panel is fixed in place with half a dozen small nails. For the sake of neatness, ensure that the top of the panel is in line with the top of the door before fixing it in place.

Because the house is fairly low, I haven't bothered to modify my ramp with any grooves or rungs for extra grip; trial and error may prove me wrong in this instance. Add two hinges to the bottom edge of the ramp using 12mm (½in) screws. You will have to hold the ramp up to the house in the closed position whilst attempting to mark the position of the hinges on the house. When you fix the ramp to the house, just add one screw in the first instance to that you can check the position and spacing before you commit to fixing.

Security

I used a selection of home-made turn-buckles to make fasteners for the doors. I used one on the bottom edge of the large door; one on the top left edge of the ramp door and one rotary device that could hold both entrances closed at once, situated between the ramp and the largest door. You could follow suit or use steel hook and eyes.

TREATMENT

As ducks are, generally speaking, filthy animals, it will pay to treat your house and treat it well – inside as well as out preferably.

In day-to-day mode, just use the ramp.

Plenty of access to clean the house out.

Even with regular additions of straw, duck muck will soon build up leaving a sloppy mess. If you plan on collecting eggs, you're going to have to clean the house out every few days. Treatment with something like Ronseal on the inside (floor and lower walls) will go a long way to stopping the plywood de-laminating in the damp conditions.

FURTHER SUGGESTIONS

The roof may want a covering of felt or plastic, as this project is most definitely a year-round outside object. I find glue and carpet tacks the best adhesives for fixing waterproofing to thin plywood roofs.

With any poultry or waterfowl, it pays to move the house around from time to time to give the ground around the entranceway a rest. Leaving your house on a patch that becomes a quagmire will only reduce its lifespan.

Whilst a chicken might last for seven or eight years, waterfowl live for decidedly longer. Ducks will live to fifteen years old as a matter of course; some may go in excess of twenty years. Geese will live even longer provided Christmas doesn't get them. Twenty years is not uncommon and twenty-five plus has been reported. You should endeavour to build your waterfowl houses with this longevity in mind; it could well be that the inhabitants will outlast their house.

Chapter 11

Goose House

GETTING STARTED WITH GEESE

I'm a bigger fan of geese than ducks. Unlike a duck, a goose will live quite happily without a pond and even if you have a pond, it will not spend a great deal of time in it or on it. Admittedly, a goose or two will still ruin a small pond – I know, I have one. I've been keeping geese for some years now; in the normal run of things we keep a breeding trio and incubate some of the eggs prior to letting the mothers sit themselves. I started out with geese about eight years ago by buying a flock of ten birds to fatten for Christmas. Out of those originals, my gander survives. He and I have somewhat of an understanding, although the quality of it varies somewhat according to the time of year. There are many breeds of geese but the most often seen white varieties are usually Embden cross Toulouse; this is a strain that combines both good overall finished size and speedy rate of growth. You may or may not know that a goose will live for many years, seventeen to eighteen is oft quoted but I do know people who claim well in excess of twenty. Of course, my goose-keeping expertise is mainly associated with breeding birds for the table. Geese come in many different varieties and strains and they may simply be kept as pets or for their ornamental attractiveness. A feisty gander also makes a cheap replacement for a Rottweiler.

A goose only has a narrow egg-laying window, which usually starts in about March. By about early February, the gander (ours is known as Mr Goose) is usually getting pretty bad tempered. Each goose will lay about ten

Geese will hide their eggs and before you know it they're sitting anywhere. This one chose the bottom of an electricity pole.

eggs to sit on; they say that 'a good goose sits early' but this doesn't always have its merits as I've had one snowed off her nest before now. If you remove eggs from the goose's nest, you can obtain up to thirty eggs from a bird during the short laying season. By about May the gander's temperament starts to calm down again, by the summer I can stroke him and pick him up; it's an odd and largely misunderstood cycle of goose hormones.

A goose will sit for 28–30 days. I take surplus eggs to a chap who specializes in the black art of hatching them. Don't bother trying incubation if you're a novice, it's not easy; the humidity has to be spot on. Incubated goslings have to be kept under heat for a couple of weeks; nature's way is better. When a sitting goose hatches her eggs, there is great excitement amongst the other geese who help the goslings to get around, corralling and steering them as appropriate. The gander is very protective and will often use his bill to nudge goslings that have fallen over back on to their feet again.

In order to keep geese you need plenty of grass, that's what they live on: grass, grass and more grass. Corn only comes into its own nearer to Christmas when it's fattening time. Geese will mix fairly well with other stock, be it poultry, sheep or cattle. My

Parents and their young. Goslings are susceptible to falling into water that's too deep for them and drowning.

gander will see off the least brave of the sheep. Recommended stocking densities are around sixteen birds to the acre on reasonable going. After hatching, the goslings grow at an astonishing rate. I have a goose that sat on seven eggs and hatched six. In the space of a fortnight, the goslings put on over a pound in weight.

You cannot introduce incubated geese into a flock until they are fully feathered up and able to fend off potential attacks from the adults. In total I aim to have about thirty geese ready for Christmas every year, although due to various mishaps throughout the year, this number is often optimistic to say the least. After the first week in November, the geese will be penned and have plenty of corn thrown at them. They tend to put this down as creamy yellow goose fat, wonderful for cooking and roasting spuds. Occasionally, it can be prudent to sell some geese off early, thus relieving one of the onerous plucking burden prior to Christmas. Anyone who has ever plucked geese will know what an awful job it is.

One of the benefits of keeping geese, weighed against other livestock, is that it is very rare to see a sick bird; apart from gizzard worm on enclosed, heavily stocked paddocks, there is little to go wrong. The biggest snag with keeping a flock of geese is that they seem to attract foxes from miles around. I read somewhere that it's the smell. Not a fortnight prior to writing this, I retrieved a goose unharmed from a fox after hearing its cries through the darkness. The fox only retreated twenty yards and loitered round me, circling from a safe radius, whilst looking for a way to get the goose back. As the winter nights start to draw in, it's imperative that geese and other poultry are locked up at dusk. Failure to do this will almost certainly result in losses.

In summary I'd say that in order to keep geese you need plenty of grass and a secure house to keep them in at night.

The Goose House Design

This project is designed to hold a trio or quad of average-sized geese. It is easy to clean and is low to the ground, so that the birds will find it easy to get in and out. Unlike ducks, geese have fairly substantial legs and are adept at stepping over things, so they should manage without a ramp.

CUTTING LIST AND MATERIAL REQUIREMENTS

Base

Bear in mind that a large sheet of plywood measures 8 × 4ft; in metric that's an unruly 1.22 × 2.44m. This baseboard is therefore a slice of the full width of one of these plywood sheets. The requirements for the base are as follows:

- One piece of 9mm (³⁄₈in) ply cut to 1.22 × 0.58m (48 × 22⅞in).
- Three 0.58m (22⅞in) pieces of 75 × 50mm (3 × 2in) timber are also required.

Sides

- To be cut from two pieces of 9mm (³⁄₈in) ply cut to 0.9 × 0.6m (35½ × 23⅝in).

The following pieces of 50 × 25mm (2 × 1in) batten are required:

- Two pieces cut to 0.5m (19¾in).
- Two pieces cut to 0.65m (25½in).
- Two pieces cut to 0.85m (33½in).

Roof and Back Panels

- One piece of 9mm (³⁄₈in) ply cut to 1.22 × 0.7m (48 × 27½in) – back panel.
- One piece of 9mm (³⁄₈in) ply cut to 1.28 × 0.67m (50⅜ × 26⅜in) – roof panel.
- Two 1.17m (46in) lengths of 50 × 25mm (2 × 1in) batten are required.

Frontal Timbers and Doors

- Three pieces of 9mm (³⁄₈in) ply cut to 0.87 × 0.4m (34¼ × 15¾in).

The following pieces of 50 × 25mm (2 × 1in) batten are required:

- One piece cut to 1.17m (46in).
- Two pieces cut to 0.81m (31⅞in).

Ancillary Items

A suitable selection of nails and screws and half a dozen 40mm (1½in) hinges are all that are required for the project. For most applications 30mm (1¼in) fixings are suitable, but four 75mm (3in) screws are needed as are some 12mm (½in) screws for fixing hinges to the plywood doors.

HOW TO ASSEMBLE THE HOUSE

The Baseboard

Get the project off to a start by making up the baseboard. The three lengths of timber are positioned so that their widest faces are in contact with the plywood floor sheet. Fasten one length under each end of the board and the remaining length under the middle. Use four screws per joint, driving them down through the plywood into the timber underneath.

Preparation and Fitting of the Side Panels

The side panels need a little material alteration prior to their use. Once again, they need to be modified to provide us with a lean-to roof profile. The finished side panels will measure 0.9m (35½in) at the front edge sloping down to 0.7m (27½in) at the rear edge. Thus a 200mm (8in) wedge needs removing from both of the side panels.

The pieces of batten that are listed are used to line the edges of both panels.

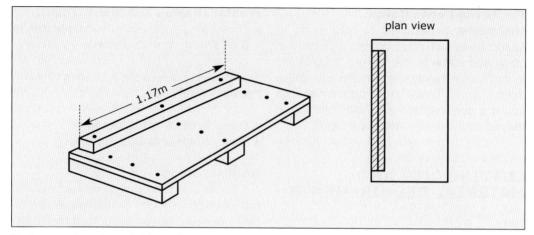

plan view

Make up a baseboard. The rail along the rear edge helps secure the back panel.

The longest pieces edge the front of the panels, the shortest lengths edge the tops and the remaining bits edge the rear. The front edge and top edge pieces are mounted so as to be flush with their respective edges. The piece of 0.65m (25½in) batten applied to the rear edge of the panel is mounted so that it is 9mm (⅜in) inward from the edge of the plywood. Both front and rear pieces are mounted so that they touch the roof line without breaking it.

The side panels can be mounted in place using four or five screws per panel. As you position each panel, you will note that it is wider than the baseboard. Fix the panels in place so that the overlap is the same, roughly 10mm (approximately ⅜in), at both sides of the panel. Screws are driven through the side panels about an inch upwards of the bottom of each panel. With the panels positioned in their respective places, the screws will catch the heavy timber supports below the baseboard.

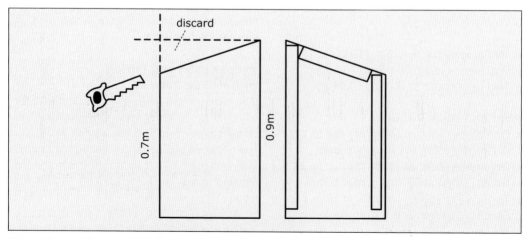

The side panels are manufactured as illustrated.

Preparation and Fitting of the Rear Panel

As the rear panel is fairly long, we've elected to add some further reinforcing pieces to it. This approach will also give us something extra to fasten the roof to. Select the two relevant lengths of 1.17m (46in) batten. One of them is mounted so that it is in a central position and flush with what will be the top edge of the sheet.

Prior to adding the back panel, an additional piece of timber is added to the rear edge of the baseboard at floor level. Site this 1.17m (46in) length so that it fits in the gap between the two side panels and is flush with the rear edge of the floor. The piece is mounted so that the narrowest 25mm (1in) face is in contact with the baseboard. Drive in screws from underneath the baseboard so that they come up through the plywood and into this length of batten.

The back panel should fit in place between the two upright ends. It can be fixed along its lower edge to the previously situated length of batten using five equally spaced 30mm (1¼in) screws. The panel is also secured to the side panels using five screws evenly spaced up each corner.

Fitting of the Front Framework

Some additional pieces of timber are required to help break up the large void at the front of the house. A horizontal bar will be used across the top of the opening with two vertical bars situated in the gap beneath, stretching down to the base unit. The top bar is a length of 1.17m (46in) batten positioned as high up as it can go without breaking the lean-to roof line. The bar is secured in place by pilot drilling and screwing two fixings at each end. Drill through the side panels and associated woodwork and into the ends of the bar; you'll need to use screws that are at least 50mm (2in) long.

Positioning of Screws

Where possible, try and position screws at regular interval so that aesthetically the project looks right. On a short side use a spacing of 100mm (4in); you can extend this to 150mm (6in) if you're running short on screws or feeling parsimonious. On longer sides, space screws at 200–250mm (8–10in). The overall aim is to make the spacing of the fixings look regular.

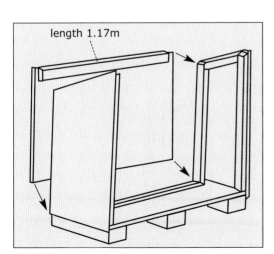

The back panel is attached to the house.

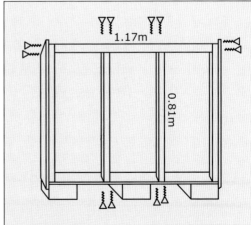

Three pieces of timber make up the framework at the front of the house.

Take a tape-measure and make marks on the baseboard for the two vertical posts. The front of the project effectively being divided into thirds, you should mark the baseboard at 407mm (16in) and 814mm (32in). These marks define the centre of each of the upright posts. Position the two posts and drill pilot holes down through the top bar and into the top of the vertical posts. Use two 75mm (3in) screws per joint. Repeat the exercise underneath the house thus fixing the bottom ends of the bars. Less substantial screws 30–40mm (1¼–1½in) can be used on these joints.

Fitting of the Roof

The roof sheet should be fixed in place using 30mm (1¼in) screws. Position the 1.28 × 0.67m (50⅜ × 26⅜in) roof panel in place and adjust it as necessary to ensure that the overlap is equal all the way around. Use four screws evenly spaced down each side and six screws at approxi-mately 200mm (8in) intervals along the front and rear sides. Ensure that your screws are positioned such as to grab the substantial timbers underneath the panel.

Fitting of the Front Panel and Doors

The front of the house consists of three ply-wood panels. The outer two panels will open on hinges and the middle panel is per-manently fixed in place. Start by adding the central panel, fixing it in place using 30mm (1¼in) screws. The panel can be secured along its top edge, down both sides, with two additional fixings at the bot-tom edge where it overlaps the baseboard support.

The doors are each fixed using three 40mm (1½in) hinges per door. The doors open like a cupboard, that is, they are hinged on opposite sides. Start by attaching the hinges to the door panels using 12mm (½in) screws. Mount the hinges 50mm (2in) inboard of the top and bottom of each

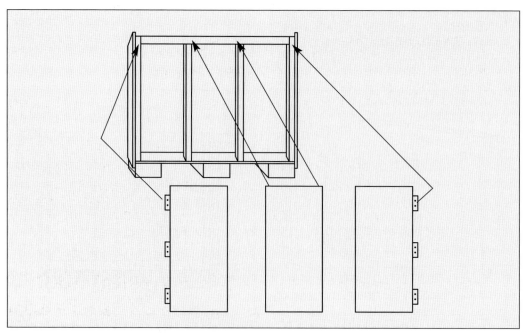

Doors and a centre panel are fixed in place.

The real thing. Don't forget to give it a lick of paint.

door; obviously, the third hinge goes in the middle of each door edge.

With the two doors made up, comes the dubious job of hanging them. Hold a door in its closed position and mark the position of the hinges against the door post. From these marks and with a little measurement you should be able to judge where the screws will go. A spare hinge can come in useful as a hole position gauge.

Always start hanging any door by just adding one or two screws to the top or bottom hinge thus allowing some leeway in aligning the rest of the door before final fixing. Aim to get the doors closing against the middle panel without leaving a large visible gap between the two panel edges.

Latches

Make a couple of wooden turn-buckle latches to keep the doors held shut. Rather than using ply off-cuts, select a 100mm (4in) length of batten and saw it in two lengthways so as to create two lengths of 25 ×

25mm (1 × 1in). Use 40–45mm (1½–1¾in) screws to fix the latches to the house. You only need one screw per latch to act as a pivot point.

TREATMENT

As with the duck house, the goose hut will require regular straw and cleaning out if it isn't going to be filled with aromatic goose slop. Likewise, I'd strongly suggest treating the floor and lower portion of the interior to help prevent rot. I've painted my hut green as it matches the goose muck. The roof can be treated, painted or given a covering, as desired.

FURTHER SUGGESTIONS

One alteration that I've thus far neglected to mention is the addition of some ventilation holes in the house. My original design

This example had minor differences. The left-hand panel was not hinged. Instead of holes, a gap was left at the top for ventilation.

got around this by leaving a gap between the roof and the tops of the front panels; the down side to this method was reduced strength in the roof. As for the duck house, find a 25mm (1in) flat-bladed drill or auger and mark a series of holes in the centre panel. You can add some in each of the doors as well if you like. Drill holes in a regular pattern and they look attractive, drill them skew whiff and they look a mess.

The first few times that you try and get your geese to go to bed, you'll have a bit of a fiasco. In all probability you'll need to herd them into a race made from sheep hurdles, gates or old pallets. After the first few times of being forced, they do get the hang of it and, although they don't have the tendency to put themselves to bed of their own accord, they will go quite readily when it starts getting dark and a well intentioned human arrives. If you do decide to keep geese, you do need decent fencing; at certain times of year they don't go well with people, certainly not children; at most times of year geese are apt to make a hell of a mess of any half-tidy garden.

Narcissus the Gander

Some years ago, a goose drowned itself in a drain. The lonesome gander wandered around forlornly until he met a companion in the yard. Unfortunately that companion was a half-decent motor with very shiny paint. It took a while for me to work out why the paint had suddenly become completely knackered on one corner of the car. After parting him from his own reflection, we got him another two ladies.

Chapter 12

Brooder Box for Rearing Chicks

THE INS AND OUTS OF HATCHING CHICKS

A brooder box is used for rearing newly hatched chicks. You would need a brooder box if you intend to try your hand at breeding poultry. 'Well' I hear you say, 'I've only got three chickens and I don't know how to breed them' – read on, dear friend; I started with four ex-battery chickens and now I have a thousand pigs.

The trouble with chickens is that they are addictive, there are a huge array of colours, shapes and sizes, and so inevitably two or three birds are never enough. Some time after experiencing the lovely fresh eggs with their bright yellow yolks, one's mind tends to drift towards having chicks and incubation. For those of you who, for whatever reason, can't have or don't desire a cockerel, it's not hard to find someone locally who will sell you a few fertile eggs; failing that, attend a poultry auction where boxes of fertile eggs from specified breeds and breeders are aplenty.

The reasons for using an incubator over and above a hen are many and varied. Firstly, you may not have a broody hen or it may be too early in the year for hens to want to sit. Then there's the numbers game: a chicken might comfortably manage eight or ten eggs, an incubator will manage whatever it's been designed to hold. Some birds and breeds of fowl are great mothers;

others are not. It's very difficult for a hen that's hatched ten chicks to keep her brood through to maturity; rats, stoats, weasels, hedgehogs and other birds are but some of the predators the young chicks will face. There's definitely nothing like nature's way but the attrition rate is generally higher than what you'd expect from a carefully monitored electric breeding setup.

Which Incubator?

When selecting an incubator, you must first decide how many eggs you want to incubate at a time. Please bear in mind at this stage the following basic statistics. Out of an incubator load of eggs, a 70–80 per cent hatch rate is pretty good; however, 50–60 per cent is normal with many small cheaper machines. There are occasions when you may not even achieve a 30 per cent success rate. If we take 60 per cent as a happy medium, then bear in mind that the hatch will include cocks. I had a strain of Lavender Araucana where the cock to hen ratio was constantly up around 70:30. With such very poor ratios out of an incubator load of some forty-two eggs, I was getting about half a dozen hens every time.

The point is this, there are occasions when you get great hatch rates and loads of hens, but equally the reverse applies. Don't choose a tiny, cheap incubator that minimizes your chances of breeding anything useful. I'd purchase a machine that holds at least forty eggs; you can always sell off the excess birds. Incubators come in a huge variety of shapes, colours and prices. I have learnt the hard way that you get what you pay for.

During incubation, the critical factors are temperature and humidity. Atmospheric pressure also disturbs the process, although this can't be helped. The temperature-controlling electronics or mechanism is the crucial part of most incubators and it is for this that your money is spent. Temperature control is the fundamental basis of an incubator and whilst it is fair to say that the other ingredient is correct humidity, the second cannot be obtained without the first. Chicken eggs generally incubate over a 21-day period and require a steady temperature of 37.5°C (100°F). Traditional incubators often worked on some sort of partially evacuated capsule that would expand and contract as the temperature in the incubator altered; this in turn altered a mechanical linkage thus controlling the heat source. Modern incubators rely on electronic temperature control and nowadays employ an electric heat source instead of a paraffin heater. The first incubator I bought was not electronically controlled, it had a set of bellows that expanded according to internal temperature. I soon discovered that the temperature fluctuated across about 5° and you had to learn how to adjust the machine so that the eggs were at the mid-point of this variation band. After a time, I upgraded to a Brinsea incubator of similar size but with electronic temperature control – what a difference! Although the machine cost a lot more money, the hatch rates increased substantially. Whilst this is not a sponsored plug for one particular company, digital temperature control certainly helps. I believe digital humidity control is now also available but at a substantial cost.

The other desirable function that should be mentioned is automatic turning. If you watch a sitting hen for long enough, you will discover that periodically she will rise from her nest for food and water and also to re-arrange her eggs. There's a purpose to this re-arrangement, the developing embryos require movement to prevent them remaining stagnant in the egg. If an embryo were to develop without movement, the weight of the embryo pressing against the inside of the shell produces deformation and eventually death. The point at which the embryo rests against the shell needs to be altered, this movement aids even embryonic development. As a speculative purchaser you can turn eggs by hand once a day or purchase a model that turns automatically. In effect, either the whole automatic incubator will either seesaw gently or contain a set of egg trays that will move in a similar fashion.

Perhaps the last criterion worth considering is that there are two basic types of incubator: forced air and still air. Still-air models rely on convection to circulate the heat; forced air models achieve a more even temperature distribution throughout the incubator by the use of a fan. I have converted a still-air model and found that the hatch rate improved with a small internal fan. Cheap 12V computer fans are ideal for this application and allow a more even spread of warm air throughout the incubator.

The Incubation Process

Egg fertility cannot be guaranteed purely by the fact that there is a cock with the hens. All laying birds should be in good health with a nice sheen on their feathers. It is unwise to select birds for breeding that carry poor markings, abnormalities or are just generally poor egg-layers (unless that is indicative of the breed). If you see the cock bird up to his business, then there is a good chance that freshly laid eggs will be fertile. If you have never incubated eggs before, there are a series of measures that you should take that will markedly improve your incubation success rate, these are as follows:

1. Eggs are fertile for up to three weeks after they have been laid, 2–14 days is best.
2. Wash the eggs in an egg disinfectant before incubation for optimum results.
3. The eggs should have been left indoors to acclimatize to room temperature before use.
4. The incubator should not be positioned in an area of variable temperature, such as a windowsill.
5. The incubator should be run up to operating temperature and adjusted correctly before introducing eggs.
6. The eggs need turning daily, gently and quickly so the overall temperature doesn't reduce.
7. Candle the eggs at seven days and discard those that are not fertile.
8. At day 19 (chicken eggs) introduce a water tray into the incubator and maintain its contents; close off the top ventilation holes, the water will evaporate and increase the humidity for hatching.

During the incubation process, regular temperature monitoring is important as it takes very little variation to kill the developing embryos. If the incubator does not have a digital readout, monitoring can only be done successfully with a thermometer inside the incubator. A small plastic window in the lid allows one to see inside and, if a small thermometer is left inside the incubator, the internal temperature can easily be read. It is of interest to note that in the latter stages of development, the unhatched chick starts producing its own heat; eggs en masse, this may lead to an undesirable rise in overall temperature in some incubators. Stay vigilant and make (tiny) adjustments as necessary.

Quick Egg Candling

It is important to candle your precious cargo at about a week to check for development of the embryo. Traditional candling of eggs was done in a darkened room in front of... yes, you've guessed it, a candle. Times may have moved on but squinting at an egg in front of a bright light in a dark room still remains the favoured way of checking fertility and embryo development. Cut a piece of board so it's big enough to sit over the lens of a bright halogen torch or it will completely block the light from a metal desk lamp. Drill a hole the size of a five-pence piece in the middle of your board, the egg will be candled by placing it over this narrow light source. Either carefully juggle the whole affair or tape the board in place. What you are looking for is a system of blood vessels emerging from the developing embryo. Discard eggs you are certain are infertile as they tend to break, crack, explode or generally make a stinking nuisance of themselves later on.

Rearing Chicks

If you've got it right, then the first indications of your reward may be the cheeps and squeaks emitted from still un-pipped eggs. Don't be fooled waiting for the exact day, some of my recent hatches have come as early as nineteen days after they were first put into the machine. As soon as there is any indication of hatching, try and raise the humidity in the incubator if you have not done so already. Also remember to remove all egg supports and turning apparatus. As the eggs start to hatch, leave the machine alone so that the humidity stays high. After hatching, chicks should stay in the incubator or similar heated brooder for up to twenty-four hours; during this time there is no requirement for them to eat or drink as they already have food in their stomachs to last them through this period. I occasionally reach in and remove egg shells if things start to look a bit cramped. If a chick does look dried out and healthy before twenty-four hours have expired, they don't take any harm going straight into a box under a lamp. What you will find is that the bulk of the hatch will occur within five or six hours; inevitably there are eggs that are still unhatched or partially hatched. Whilst assisting the stragglers is rarely recommended, it is these guys that end up welded to their shells as the gunk around them sets rock hard once they've partially opened their egg. I have saved one or two by helping them out, the tail-end Charlies often have leg-related and other deformities, and you end up having to cull them anyway.

Unless you have a vast number of chicks, don't bother with large heat lamps, 100W reflector bulbs are just as effective and cheaper to run. Use plastic storage containers to start with, and put sand or sawdust in the bottom to absorb droppings. Chicks should be fed on chick crumb, which can be placed in ramekins, cut-off plastic bottles or proper feeders. I generally put pebbles in the drinking pots so that the water is not deep enough for the chicks to drown in and they can clamber out again. The plastic storage containers might do for a week or so, then it's off to a much larger plywood brooder box in the shed; the high sides of this wooden box also reduce the metaphorical chances of rats and cats amongst the pigeons. At between four and six weeks old, depending on size, start feeding the young chickens a growers ration instead of chick crumb.

The Brooder Box Design

There are two variations on this design corresponding to indoor and outdoor use. Essentially, the indoor brooder box requires a full floor, whereas the outdoor variety only requires a partial floor in the sleeping area. The basic element of the project is the construction of a large deep rectangular box. This on its own would be a useful asset for

rearing chicks. By the addition of an enclosed sleeping area, we have something that could be used outside with a small heat lamp inside it.

CUTTING LIST AND MATERIAL REQUIREMENTS

The box is made without any additional bracing timber and is therefore made out of 12mm (½in) plywood. Although a lot heavier than 9mm (⅜in) ply, this gauge of timber allow the joints of the box to be drilled and screwed together without additional means of reinforcement. The internal divider and lid are made from 9mm (⅜in) ply.

Base
- One piece of 12mm (½in) ply cut to 1.195 × 0.61m (47 × 24in).

Sides
- Two pieces of 12mm (½in) ply cut to 1.22 × 0.45m (48 × 17¾in).

Sides
- Two pieces of 12mm (½in) ply cut to 0.61 × 0.45m (24 × 17¾in).

Partition
- To be cut from one piece of 9mm (⅜in) ply cut to 0.6 × 0.425m (23⅝ × 16¾in).

The following pieces of 50 × 25mm (2 × 1in) batten are required:

- One piece cut to 0.39m (15⅜in).
- One piece cut to 0.6m (23⅝in).
- One piece cut to 0.195m (7⅞in).

Sleeping Area Roof
- Two pieces of 9mm (⅜in) ply cut to 0.39 × 0.19m (15⅜ × 7½in).
- One piece of 9mm (⅜in) ply cut to 0.63 × 0.20m (24¾ × 7⅞in).

- One piece of 9mm (⅜in) ply cut to 0.63 × 0.40m (24¾ × 15¾in).

Run Lid and Supports

- One piece of 9mm (⅜in) ply cut to 0.3 × 0.63m (12 × 24¾in).
- One piece of 50 × 25mm (2 × 1in) batten cut to 0.6m (23⅝in).

Ancillary Items

The lid is held together with polyurethane

> ### Pilot Drilling Holes
>
> The drill needs to leave a hole with a smaller diameter than the screw. For most of these projects a 2.5mm (about ³⁄₃₂in) pilot drill is fine. Aim to drill the holes 6mm (¼in) inboard of the edges of the ply so that they cut into the core of the baseboard sheet.

(PU) wood glue and the rest of the project is secured with 30mm screws. A piece of chicken wire is required for the top with a few galvanized staples to hold it in place. Four hinges are required to secure the nesting box roof and the access door to the run.

HOW TO ASSEMBLE THE PROJECT

Box

Lay the base panel on the floor. The other components are fixed around this panel. Position the other panels against the floor panel, they do not sit on top of it. Start by positioning an end piece against the base panel. Use an electric drill to pilot drill a couple of holes along the joint; go through the panel and into the baseboard. Put in two fastenings and then drill another four

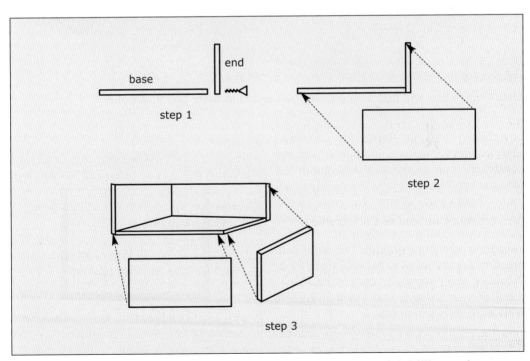

Cut the required panels to size and start building your box. Careful drilling and screwing is required along the edges to avoid splitting the plywood.

A well-made box will last a long time. This one is at least five years old.

holes along the joint. Rather than immediately adding the second end panel, turn the construction on its side and add one of the side panels. This will make the construction more rigid and easier to work with. Remember to pilot drill holes and add screws every 200mm (8in) or so.

Add the remaining end and the other side in a similar manner as previously described. Providing you have taken care in the placement of your screws, you will now be left with a strong wooden box.

Partition

The partition is cut from one piece of 9mm (⅜in) ply cut to 0.6 × 0.425m (23⅝ × 16¾in).

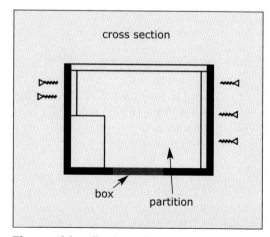

The partition fits into the box as illustrated in this cross-sectional view of the project.

Partition on the right, sleeping area roof on the left.

This piece needs minor alteration by way of a doorway adding. Bearing in mind that the shortest side is the height of the partition and the longest side will fit in the width of the box: cut out a corner that is 120mm (4¾in) wide and 200mm (8in) high.

Hold the panel so that the doorway is on the left. The lengths of batten are now added to the far side of the panel as follows:

- The piece cut to 0.6m (23⅝in) is fitted flush with the top edge of panel.
- The 0.39m (15⅜in) batten is fitted down the 0.6 × 0.425m (16¾in) side.
- The remaining piece is fitted down the side above the doorway; 0.195m (7⅝in).

The partition can now be fitted in place. Position the divider so that there is a 360mm (14⅛in) gap between an end wall of the box and the batten on the back of the partition. The smaller enclosed area created by the partition will be the warm sleeping

The partition has been fixed in place, a bar added to provide support for a run door and some wire mesh has been fastened to the top.

area. The divider can be fixed in place by driving screws through the sides of the box into the partition. The screws should catch the bracing pieces on the partition.

Run Lid and Supports

An opening lid can be made from a piece of 9mm (⅜in) ply cut to 0.3 × 0.63m (12 × 24¾in). Add two hinges to the piece of ply using 12mm (½in) screws. By adding a length of 0.6m (23⅝in) batten across the width of the brooder box, we'll have something to attach the lid to. This piece of batten will fit across the box (in-between the side panels). Use the lid as a template and position it over the open end of the box (not

The run door in the closed position. The sleeping compartment roof is on.

the smaller partitioned end). Screw the bar in place according to where the hinges on the lid lie. As a guide, there should be about 270mm (10⅝in) between the end of the box and the bar. The bar will need two screws in each end to keep it steady.

Looking at the top of the box, there will be an apparent middle section between the newly installed lid and the partition that can be covered in fine chicken wire. If you are intending to treat or paint the box, do it prior to adding the mesh covering.

Sleeping Area Roof

The run door is fixed in place, no excuses for the recycled piece of plywood.

The sleeping area roof is mildly convoluted and so, to lessen the burden of manufacture,

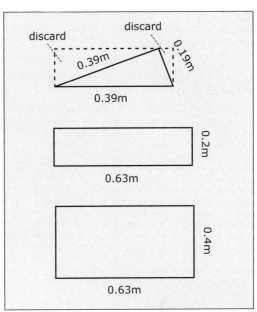

Cut out the illustrated components, which are used to make the sleeping area roof.

The finished roof. The narrow pieces of plywood used to reinforce the joints can be seen on the inside of the roof.

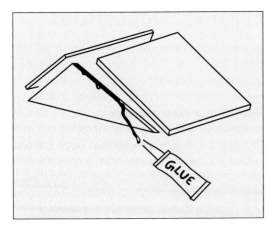

The panels are glued together as shown. Some small pieces of scrap wood are used to reinforce the seams on the inside of the roof.

has been made using pieces of ply cut to shape and held together with quick-drying glue. I used tape to hold the pieces of ply in place for the five minutes or so that it took for the glue to set. To aid strength, I used off-cuts of plywood 12mm (½in) wide and as long as necessary to line the inside of all the glued joints.

After cutting the triangles required to make the sides of the roof, start the gluing process by joining these sections to the largest of the sheets. Tape all the pieces in place and leave the project to dry. Once the glue has dried, use some more adhesive and add the second roof panel.

When the roof is finished and dry, it can have two hinges added to the shortest sloping side. These in turn are attached to the end of the brooder box so that the roof is held in place over the sleeping compartment.

The last addition to the inside of the roof was a small screw-in eye in the top of the

A small eye is screwed into the inside of the ridge. A low-powered heat lamp is tied to this eye.

roof; this will enable the securing of a small, low-powered heat lamp to help keep the chicks warm.

TREATMENT

My device is designed to be used indoors or outdoors if the weather is fair. All plywood survives best when painted. The conundrum here is what to do with the roof. As I will occasionally use my box outdoors with a heat lamp, I will waterproof the roof using felt. If you have got the seams of your roof tight, the roof may be watertight with a simple coat of wood preserver.

FURTHER SUGGESTIONS

If you want to make a box with a partial floor, you'll be able to give your poultry access to a little grass. Over the years, I've made several of these boxes and have found them extremely useful. Don't forget to throw in a little sawdust from day to day to absorb the droppings from your chicks. Hopefully the whole process hasn't sounded too onerous and got you wringing your hands in despair. For any family with young kids, incubation is quite simply a must.

The run is finished and ready for the chicks; time to start up the incubator.

Index